BEST

PRACTICES

BEHAVIORAL

AND EDUCATIONAL

STRATEGIES FOR TEACHERS

edited by

H. Kenton Reavis, Ed.D.
▼
Mae Taylor Sweeten, Ph.D.
▼
William R. Jenson, Ph.D.
▼
Daniel P. Morgan, Ph.D.
▼
Debra J. Andrews, M.S.
▼
Susan L. Fister, M.Ed.

Printed in the United States of America

06 05 04 03 02   12 11 10 9 8

ISBN 1-57035-052-3

Edited by Raven Moore
Cover design, text layout/design by Sherri Rowe

Published and Distributed by

SOPRIS
WEST
EDUCATIONAL SERVICES

4093 Specialty Place • Longmont, Colorado 80504 • (303) 651-2829 • www.sopriswest.com

79BEST / 12-02 / C&M / 1.5M / 283

Table of Contents

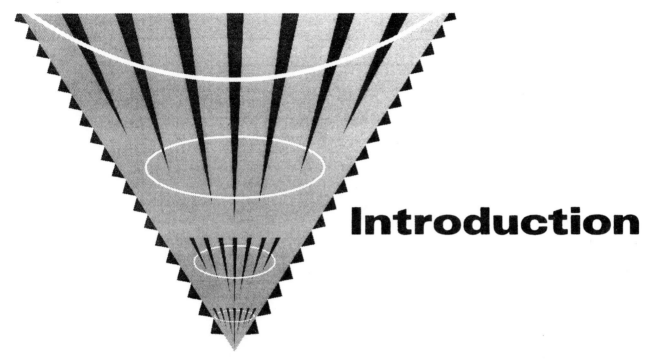

Introduction

BEST Practices is what many of today's teachers request for help in their classrooms. They want to know how to manage disruptive classroom behaviors, keep students on-task, stop noncompliance, improve students' academic performance, and improve their own positive interactions with students. This book is designed to give teachers practical information that can be used directly in classrooms to benefit students who are having difficulty.

The term "best practices" simply means that the techniques introduced in this book are based on research-validated strategies that have been shown to work with students. Not all techniques work in every situation with every student; however, the techniques presented here have been shown to work in a majority of situations with students who have difficulty with disruptive behavior and nonmotivation. Several different strategies are presented so that if one does not work, another can be tried. The techniques include self-monitoring, peer tutoring, cooperative learning, time-out, in-school suspension, advertising for success, contracting, and teacher praise, to name a few. The strategies presented are primarily positive, so that students having difficulty will be ensured a positive and successful educational experience.

Most of the strategies are given with step-by-step instructions for implementation and troubleshooting. Also included are several useful forms such as homenotes and contracts, which teachers can photocopy for use in their own classrooms. Each strategy can be used on its own or in combination with other techniques.

The original strategies developed for this book came from Utah's Behavioral and Educational Strategies for Teachers (BEST). This is an approach developed by the Utah State Office of Education in cooperation with several school districts for systems change in education for at-risk and behavior disordered students.

Advertising for Success: Improving Motivation

by William R. Jenson, Ph.D., University of Utah, and H. Kenton Reavis, Ed.D., Utah State Office of Education

Introduction

Advertising for success (also known as public posting) is an intervention that may be used to enhance academic motivation and decrease disruptive behaviors. Advertising for success primarily involves the display of academic progress scores or behavior measures on a bulletin board or blackboard. The academic measures can include such items as scores on papers, test scores, points earned for academic work, the number of assignments completed, percentage of assignments completed, contributions made in class, and other measures. Behavior measures can include such items as on-task behavior, being on time to class, being prepared to work, the number of warnings received for inappropriate behaviors, appropriate transitions from class to class, and so on.

OBJECTIVES

By the end of this module, you will know:

- What advertising for success is.
- What makes advertising for success effective.
- How to implement an advertising for success system.
- Cautions when using an advertising for success system.

Is Advertising for Success Effective?

Advertising for success is well-represented in the Effective Schools Literature. This literature has been compiled and reviewed by a number of researchers interested in the differences between effective and ineffective schools (Jenson, Sloane, & Young, 1988; Purkey & Smith, 1983). A list of the characteristics of effective schools is provided below:[*]

1. There is school-wide recognition of academic success.

2. Basic academic subjects are emphasized.

3. Clear goals and high expectations are maintained for all students.

4. There is a school-wide sense of order and discipline.

5. Teachers reward, praise, and recognize student performance.

6. The school principal provides strong leadership, which filters down through the teaching staff to the students.

7. The principal supports and encourages the staff.

8. The school has a monitoring system that reports student progress.

9. Teachers, principals, and parents are kept aware of pupils' progress relative to school objectives.

10. The amount of time students spend on engaged academic tasks is high (minimum 70%).

11. Teachers set the stage for learning at the beginning of the school year.

12. Teachers prepare students for independent inquiry and study.

13. There is widespread support from the school staff, parents, and students regarding school norms for behavior.

14. Teachers use a variety of discipline strategies for managing disruptive behavior.

15. Teachers create an environment that models high learning expectations.

16. Teachers are able to motivate children.

17. Teachers use a classroom system of rules.

18. Teachers optimize learning time.

19. Teachers move around the room, are aware of what is going on, and use a system of spot checking.

20. Teachers handle disruptive behavior in a low-key manner.

It is important to note that items 1 and 8 directly relate to advertising for success. Posting the academic scores of students provides school-wide recognition, and facilitates monitoring and reporting of student progress.

Academic increases also result from advertising for success. For example, the system has been used to improve performance in the following studies:

1. Fourth graders' science test errors were reduced from approximately 27% to 7% (Thorpe & Darch, reported in Van Houten, 1980).

2. Second graders' mean words written increased from approximately five per minute to ten per minute (Van Houten, Hill, & Parsons, 1975).

3. Special education students' (EMR eight to 12 years old) mean math lessons completed each day increased from approximately .69 to 1.3 lessons per day through team advertising for success (Van Houten & Van Houten, 1977).

4. Fifth graders' mean number of questions answered correctly about the stories in their readers increased from approximately four to eight with team advertising for success (Van Houten, 1980).

5. High school biology test performance increased from an average of 55% to 73% with advertising for success, verbal praise, and immediate feedback (Van Houten & Lai Fatt, 1981).

Other suggested areas for academic advertising for success include spelling scores, basic number facts, handwriting samples, story writing, math calculations such as long division, physical education activities, classroom verbal contributions, completed homework assignments, and others (Van Houten, 1980).

---

[*] Partially abstracted from:

Colorado Department of Education, School Improvement and Leadership Services Unit. (1982). *Indicators of quality schools.* Unpublished paper.

MacKay, A. (1982). *Project Quest: Teaching strategies and pupil achievement.* Occasional Papers Series, Centre for Research in Teaching, University of Alberta.

Purkey, S.C. & Smith, M.S. (1983). Effective schools: A review. *Elementary School Journal, 83,* 427-452.

Advertising for success has also been used to reduce disruptive classroom behavior and improve on-task classroom performance. Lyman (1984) has specifically used advertising for success and goal setting to improve the on-task behavior of elementary age (11 to 13 years), behaviorally disordered boys. All of the subjects were identified as conduct disordered and displayed such behaviors as noncompliance, aggression, truancy, and property destruction. The study took place in a self-contained classroom at a treatment center. The treatment initially involved having the boys set their own goals for on-task behavior and write them privately on index cards, which the teacher kept at her desk. The effects were not impressive. However, when the boys' goals were transferred to an advertising for success chart there was a large increase in on-task behavior (from 50% to 75%). Clearly, public posting of the goals was a critical variable for improving on-task behavior.

In a similar study, Jones and Van Houten (1985) used public posting of daily quiz results in science and English to manage disruptive behavior in three junior high school classrooms. The quizzes were simple five-question tests (true or false, fill in the blank, or multiple choice) on the subject content and were administered during the last five minutes of each class. It is interesting to note that at no time was there a public posting of disruptive behavior. At first, data on disruptive behavior were collected only when quizzes were started. This produced a reduction in disruptive behavior in classes 1 and 3, but not 2.

The test scores were recorded on a large wall chart in black grease crayon. Students were told that the purpose of the chart was to see if each student could exceed his/her previous best daily and weekly score. With the introduction of public posting of quiz results, there was a large reduction in disruptive behavior (from approximately 40% to 10%) without the implementing of additional disciplinary procedures.

> Since most advertising for success sytems have no tangible reward or reinforcement associated with the student's performance, the reaction of others (particularly peers) is very important. Engineering reactions is a skill that needs to be mastered by teachers who use an advertising for success system.

What Makes Advertising for Success Effective?

Whether it is used for improving academics or behavior, there are a number of essential components that must be present in order for advertising for success to be effective.

First, the basic component of all public posting systems involves some type of visual feedback system. This must be something students can see from their desks. A large bulletin board, marks on the blackboard, or a plastic-covered or laminated poster board are all good places to post visual feedback systems.

Second, the advertising for success system needs accurate and meaningful information that can be displayed. This requires some systematic method of gathering information. The more delayed or the less accurate the information, then the less effective the public posting system. Collecting relevant information is the key to advertising for success; conscientious teachers can readily collect this information and use it. There are several efficient techniques that will be discussed later in this module on how to collect meaningful information for display.

The third component of an advertising for success system is the engineered reaction to the information. This aspect can be critical to the success or failure of the system. Engineered reactions are the responses of teachers, aides, the principal, and peers to the information included in an advertising for success system. Since most of these systems have no tangible reward or reinforcement associated with the student's performance, the reaction of others (particularly peers) is very important. Engineering reactions is a skill that needs to be mastered by teachers who use an advertising for success system. Details on this skill will be given later in this module.

Steps for Implementing Advertising for Success

The steps for implementing an advertising for success system have been described in a book entitled _Learning Through Feedback: A Systematic Approach for Improving Academic Performance_ (Van Houten, 1980). The following steps for implementing an advertising for success system were abstracted from this book and from other supporting material.

STEP ONE

Select a visual feedback system that will be prominently displayed in the classroom. The display should be large enough to be seen by students sitting at their desks. For example, the lettering of names and performance information or data should be at least three centimeters high. The chart should also display a week's worth of data (Monday through Friday) with each student's highest weekly score. The charts should be erasable so they can be re-used each week. A poster board covered with a plastic film or lamination is best. It is also very important to keep the visual feedback system simple. The more complex the system, the less it will be used by students. Too much information, small graphs, or complex measures will reduce the effectiveness of advertising for success.

STEP TWO

Decide on a positive measure. It is important to post improvements and not setbacks. The research has shown that posting positive improvements is much more effective than posting measures that indicate poor performance or inappropriate behavior. A positive measure is also one in which a student is compared against his/her own performance and not the performance of other students. If students are routinely compared against each other, then the poorer-performing students will find the procedure punishing.

STEP THREE

Decide on meaningful and precise daily measures. For example, measures such as number of problems completed, percentage of improvement, points earned for appropriate behavior, or words read are all good ones. Global measures, or information that is dependent on guesswork, is poor information to post.

STEP FOUR

Give feedback immediately. The longer a teacher waits to give feedback to a student, the less effective the advertising for success system will be. Therefore, feedback should be given as soon as possible.

STEP FIVE

Develop a system to effectively score students' work so that it can be posted immediately. The usual reason that feedback is delayed to students is that teachers do not have time to immediately grade or evaluate academic work. A way to overcome this problem is to use student graders or self-grading. Research has shown that self-grading can be effectively used in a classroom and that students learn even more from self-grading (Van Houten, 1980) than from having someone else grade their work. Three sample methods for self-grading are:

Method 1

Give the students specially colored pencils or pens that can only be used for grading when the answers are given orally to the group by the teacher. Any student using a regular pencil during grading can be readily identified as cheating. The teacher may also randomly sample some of the papers and grade them for accuracy after the students have graded them.

Method 2

Set up grading stations in the classroom with the answer sheets and a special red pencil for grading. The student is allowed to bring only his/her answer sheet to the grading station. No pencils or other papers are allowed.

Method 3

Have students exchange papers and put their initials at the bottom of the paper as a grader. It will also help to have students rotate the papers, once, twice, or three times so the student does not know who is grading his/her paper. Again, a teacher can randomly grade three or four papers as a reliability check.

STEP SIX

Give positive differential feedback rather than feedback for an absolute level or near perfect goal. With positive differential feedback, students post improvements against their own best scores and not against a predetermined criterion. For example, if a student's best score for completing math problems any day during the present week is 20 and his/her best score ever for any week is 35, then these scores would be posted as follows:

Student	M	T	W	TH	F	Best Day	Best Week
J. Doe	15	13	20	18	—	20	35

In this way, students compete against themselves.

STEP SEVEN

The teacher should praise improvements on the advertising for success chart. This is what makes the information meaningful and reinforcing to students. The teachers should use descriptive praise statements such as: "John, what a performance! You beat your best weekly score again!"; or "Susan is getting better and better; she did six more problems today!" Poor praise statements are global ones such as: "Good job, keep it up," or "Nice improvement."

It is also important to praise students who are having difficulty, but are improving. Small steps are particularly important to these students, and their performance should always be compared to their own previous work (e.g., "Wow, Timmy is really doing a great job. If you look at his chart, he has improved each day. I have to keep changing his Best Day score.").

Group praise is also effective if it is used descriptively and does not single out students who are having difficulty. Good group praise statements are: "This is impressive; six students in this class beat their previous best scores," or "What a hot class, you beat your total class best score again—what a bunch of pros."

It is a good idea for teachers to set goals for the number of praise statements that they will make during each day about the publicly posted information. For example, a teacher may set the minimum number of praise statements at ten for himself/herself and five for the classroom aide. This may seem artificial at first; however, it will eventually pay off. It helps to post the number on the blackboard, with

> Research indicates that if students compete against themselves and not each other, spontaneous student comments will be positive.

only the teacher and aide knowing what the number means. Research has shown that when teachers publicly post the number of praise statements they make, the number goes up (Gross & Ekstrand, 1983).

STEP EIGHT

Encourage peer comments and interaction about the posted information. Research indicates that if students compete against themselves and not each other, spontaneous student comments will be positive (Van Houten, 1980). However, if students compete against each other, the chances of negative or counter-productive comments increase. A teacher can also foster positive student comments in the following ways:

Method 1

Acknowledging students' comments. For instance, a student (John) might say, "Timmy beat his best score." The teacher's remark might be, "John, you are sharp for noticing; Timmy is doing a great job."

Method 2

Amplifying a student's positive comment by adding information. For example, a student might say, "Charlie really did a good job today." The teacher might comment, "He did an additional 12 problems and beat his own best score."

Method 3

Praising a student for making positive comments about other students. A teacher might say to a student who has just made a positive comment, "Susan, you are terrific at noticing how well others are doing on the chart. Your comments make everyone feel good."

Method 4

Using confederates to stimulate peer comments about publicly posted information. For example, a teacher may directly ask two or three popular students in the class to make positive comments about how other students are doing. The teacher should stress that the comments should be sincere and realistic. Having socially valued, popular peers make comments is contagious, and other students will also start to make positive comments.

While the eight basic steps for designing and operating an advertising for success system have been detailed previously, there are several advanced techniques that can further improve the effects of a well-designed and well-implemented system.

ADVANCED TECHNIQUE ONE

Add a tangible reinforcer for students who have improved their scores. This seems simple, but remember that the system that has been presented so far in this module has only used teacher and peer praise as reinforcement for improvement. Mystery motivators, spinners, grab bags, or treasure boxes can be used randomly to reinforce students. For instance, a student can be selected at random from those who have posted improvements for a particular day. This student receives the daily mystery motivator (a sealed envelope posted at the front of the class containing a reinforcer written on a slip of paper).

Caution: It is important to select an improving student at random. Do not make the reinforcer dependent on the biggest improvement. If the reinforcers are given only to students making the biggest gains, then students who are having more difficulty but who are improving will be punished.

ADVANCED TECHNIQUE TWO

Some teachers have difficulty grading papers and posting all the students' work each day. To solve this problem, the teacher can post a chart with several spaces for students' names and can randomly select students at the end of the day to have their work graded and the information posted. With this technique, students are never sure who will have their work posted, so all students work hard.

Van Houten's report of Thorpe and Darch's study (1980) describes a random selection technique in which one fourth grade student's daily science test was randomly selected and scored by the teacher. The test was posted on the board in front of the class if it had no more than one error. If the test had more than one error, the student remained anonymous and no test was posted. Errors dropped dramatically with this technique from an average of 28% to less than 10%.

It is important to randomly select students for posting. Singling students out for advertising for success because they are doing poorly can be a punishing experience.

ADVANCED TECHNIQUE THREE

Classrooms can be divided into teams and average team results can be posted. For example, three students sitting at a table for math can be designated as a team. At the end of each math period, the students can exchange papers with each other or even with another team for grading. The amount of each assignment correctly completed (number of problems) can be averaged and the team's performance can be posted along with their best daily score and best weekly score. A team approach does not require that individual names be posted, only a team name. However, both team and individual performance can be posted together, if desired.

Van Houten and Van Houten (1977) used individual versus individual plus team posting with elementary age, special education students. They found that team posting was superior to individual posting, but that both approaches improved performance. In using individual posting, the increase was from .69 math assignments to .84 reading assignments completed, an increase of 22%. However, when team as well as individual results were posted, the increase was from .69 reading assignments to 1.30 reading assignments, an increase of 61%. Interestingly, the percentage of spontaneous positive remarks made by the students about the reading work jumped from a baseline of 0 to 31.7 comments per day.

Performance can also be enhanced by using an advertising for success system that displays several behaviors and academic skills for a whole class instead of only one behavior or skill for individual students. On the form at the end of this module, **the triangles on the upper right of the page** represent four classroom rules pertaining to: (1) Correct transition time, (2) Accuracy of following directions, (3) Work completed, and (4) No more than one warning.

These behaviors are tracked for the class for the academic subjects of math, reading, and spelling. If the class performs appropriately during an academic period, a plus (+) is placed in each area. If

Singling students out for advertising for success because they are doing poorly can be a punishing experience.

misbehavior occurs, then a minus (-) is placed in that particular area. The advantage of this system is the simplicity of posting for the whole class across several behaviors. The publicly posted behaviors in this example represent the standard class rules, and the teacher can combine the advertising for success system with an incentive system.

ADVANCED TECHNIQUE FOUR

An even more powerful application of advertising for success is to combine it with a team-based group contingency. With a group contingency, the classroom is divided into teams as described previously; however, a reward or contingency is added for team performance. This technique was used effectively with 254 primary and middle school students who displayed high rates of misbehavior (swearing, gum chewing, entering school without permission, talking back, running in hallways, loitering, kicking, fighting) (Hollan & McLaughlin, 1982). Each class was given ten points each day (each class formed a team). If a student misbehaved, he/she lost one point from the class's total. The publicly posted information consisted of the points remaining and the misbehavior that had caused a point loss. If a class had 45 points or more remaining at the end of the week, they were declared Class of the Week (more than one class could win). The Class of the Week winners were announced on the public address system, their class picture was posted along with their point total in the hallways, and they were awarded a large ribbon and a certificate. The class that won most often over the entire study's time was also given a free lunch. The results showed that before the intervention the primary school students had 31 inappropriate behaviors; this dropped to four after the intervention was started. Similarly, the intermediate age students had an average of 33 misbehaviors before the intervention and only five after the intervention.

Group contingencies are powerful techniques. When group contingencies are used with advertising for success, only team scores should be posted, and the teacher should be absolutely sure that all the students on the team can perform the required academic or behavioral task. Group contingencies are best used when students have learned a new behavior and need to practice it (maintenance); they are much less effective when students are still learning how to perform the behavior but have not quite mastered it (acquisition). In addition, the group contingency should be designed so that all the teams can win and the contingency is primarily a positive

procedure. The teacher can tell if the procedure is positive by asking: (1) Does a variety of teams win the contingency often? and (2) Do the students make positive comments to each other about their performance, or are they singling out a few students for ridicule?

Cautions

A visual feedback system, meaningful information, and positive reactions to the information are the essential components of advertising for success. Even though all of these elements exist in all classrooms as untapped resources, some teachers are reluctant to use advertising for success systems. For example, some teachers may express a concern that students will feel uncomfortable if their work is displayed. The research shows that most students prefer an advertising for success system if it is used correctly (Van Houten, 1980). It is important to post positive information if possible. The more negative the information, the less effective the system will be.

Other teachers are worried that slower learners will be exposed and negatively affected by the system. Students already know who are the fast and slow learners in a classroom (this is particularly true if teachers group students by ability—e.g., bluebird and blackbird reading groups). If an advertising for success system is designed correctly, it can be used to enhance the self-esteem of slow learners. In fact, research shows that students who are below average in academic rankings benefit and improve most by the system (Van Houten, 1984).

Some teachers express a concern about legal issues associated with advertising for success. While some caution is in order, the posting of students' work has been going on in classrooms for decades. However, posting should not be used to humiliate a student or to display only negative information. It is also a good idea for the teacher to inform parents at Back-To-School Night how he/she plans to conduct the posting, and to emphasize that it is a positive system. The teacher will want to explain that he/she will not be posting academic grades, but rather improvement or the number or amount of assignments completed.

The principal's permission and support should also be obtained. For example, the principal may be asked to come into the classroom periodically and look at or make comments about the advertising for success systems. One principal went so far as to take a Polaroid® picture of one student from each classroom who had done exceptionally well. Each picture, with an appropriate label such as "Incredible Worker," or "One of the Best On-Task Kids," was then posted outside of the office in the main school foyer.

If the teacher is concerned about posting names, secret number codes can be assigned instead. One study showed that posting academic progress by code is just as effective for secondary students as is posting by name (Van Houten, 1984).

References

Gross, A.M. & Ekstrand, M. (1983). Increasing and maintaining rates of teacher praise: A study using public posting and feedback fading. *Behavior Modification, 7*(1), 126-135.

Hollan, E.L. & McLaughlin, T.F. (1982). Using advertising for success to manage student behavior during supervision. *Journal of Educational Research, 76*(1), 29-34.

Jenson, W.R., Sloane, H.N., & Young, K.R. (1988). *Applied behavior analysis in education: A structured teaching approach.* Englewood Cliffs, NJ: Prentice Hall.

Jones D. & Van Houten, R. (1985). The use of daily quizzes and public posting to decrease disruptive behavior of secondary school students. *Education and Treatment of Children, 8*(2), 91-106.

Lyman, R. (1984). The effect of private and public goal setting on classroom on-task behavior of emotionally disturbed children. *Behavior Therapy, 15,* 395-402.

Purkey, S.C. & Smith, M.S. (1983). Effective schools: A review. *Elementary School Journal, 83,* 427-52.

Thorpe, H.W. & Darch, C.B. (in press). A simplified reinforcement technique for improving test accuracy. *Psychology in the Schools.*

Van Houten, R. (1980). *Learning through feedback: A systematic approach for improving academic performance.* New York: Human Sciences Press.

Van Houten, R. (1984). Setting up feedback systems in the classroom. In W.L. Heward, T.E. Herson, D.S. Hill, & J. Trap-Porter (Eds.), *Focus on behavior analysis in education.* Columbus, OH: Merrill.

Van Houten, R., Hill, S., & Parsons, M. (1975). An analysis of a performance feedback system: The effects of timing and feedback, advertising for success, and praise upon academic performance and peer interaction. *Journal of Applied Behavior Analysis, 8,* 449-457.

Van Houten, R. & Lai Fatt, D. (1981). The effects of advertising for success on high school biology test performance. *Education and Treatment of Children, 4,* 217-225.

Van Houten, R. & Van Houten J. (1977). The performance feedback system in the special education classroom: An analysis of advertising for success and peer comments. *Behavior Therapy, 8*(2), 336-376.

Whole Class Performance

Class Rules

1. Correct transition time (move quietly, go directly to the next activity).
2. Follow the teacher's directions.
3. Complete your work and keep busy for the entire class period.
4. No more than one warning.

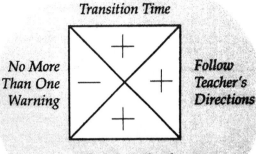

Number of Plusses

	Mon.	Tues.	Wed.	Thur.	Fri.	Best Score
Math						
Reading						
Spelling						

Best Number of Plusses for a Day

	Math	Reading	Spelling
Team 1			
Team 2			
Team 3			
Team 4			
Team 5			

Cooperative Learning

by Susan L. Fister, M.Ed., Education 1st, Salt Lake City, Utah

Introduction

Coooperative learning refers to a type of peer-mediated instruction in which small groups of students work together to help each other achieve academic and social goals.

Features of Cooperative Learning

1. Heterogeneous learning groups. Students work in small groups comprised of different ability levels, sexes, races, and backgrounds.

2. Positive interdependence. A "sink or swim together" attitude promotes the idea that students need each other to accomplish a mutual goal.

3. Individual accountability. Each group member is responsible for ultimately mastering the material.

4. Group processing. Processing activities are built into the content aspect of cooperative groups in order to continually assess important dynamics such as how the group is working together, what is going well, what needs to be improved, how well the group is functioning, etc.

OBJECTIVES

By the end of this module, you will know:

- What cooperative learning is.
- Features and benefits of cooperative learning.
- How to implement two different cooperative learning structures.

5. Social skills. Important life and job skills are taught, role played, and reinforced through collaborative group work.

6. Face to face interaction. Achievement of outcomes is due in large part to the active involvement, articulation, interaction, and explaining of concepts, skills and processes by each member of the group.

7. Group goals and reward structures. Group and/or individual rewards for a group product can be arranged to give students incentives to complete a task. Students often feel more aligned with the mainstream and are more motivated if the group is depending on their performance.

> Cooperative learning has clearly been shown to produce improvements in both academic and social relations.

Studies have noted benefits for students with disabilities. Social acceptance has been shown to improve, although, in some studies, friendships and liking did not improve. Cooperative techniques, however, have great potential for building social relationships among all students by incorporating a more aggressive peer interaction approach. Unmotivated students have shown gains in academic achievement along with increases in self-esteem and liking of school. Social isolates have been shown to increase their interaction in collaborative efforts, encounter less rejection by peers, and experience some long-term benefits in terms of social interactions with classmates. Cooperative learning has clearly been shown to produce improvements in both academic and social relations (Lovitt et. al.).

Slavin (1983) has noted that cooperative learning has the greatest impact on achievement levels when group reward structures and task specialization are in place. Combining group rewards with individual learning improves the classroom climate. Peer groups will support and nurture high achievement, often providing the necessary motivation for previously unmotivated students to excel. Students working together toward a common goal will more likely encourage each other to perform so that the entire group will benefit (Slavin, 1983).

Benefits of Cooperative Learning

1. Higher on-task behaviors, achievement, and increased retention of skills.

2. Greater opportunity for practice and use of cognitive skills such as understanding, applying, analyzing, synthesizing and evaluating information.

3. Increased motivation for task completion.

4. More opportunities for relationship building, use of communication skills, and use of social skills.

5. Improved interpersonal, collaborative, and problem solving skills.

6. Improved attitudes toward school and school personnel.

7. Fewer disruptions during academic learning time.

Is Cooperative Learning Effective?

Research in cooperative learning conducted by Johnson, Maruyama, Johnson, Nelson, and Skon (1981) has shown that cooperation is superior to competition strategies in terms of promoting achievement and productivity. Cooperation has also been shown to be superior to individualistic approaches in which students are rewarded for their individual efforts and outcomes.

Basics of Implementing Cooperative Learning

1. Identify, clearly articulate, and verify with students the academic (content) and collaborative (process) objectives for the lesson.

2. Carefully make decisions regarding the placement of students in cooperative learning groups (i.e., size, members, materials, location, roles, etc.).

3. Assess the current classroom arrangements in terms of incentive and task structures. If the classroom does not have a group or team reward system in place, then choose a reward structure that will best meet the needs of students.

4. Thoroughly explain and demonstrate to the students the expected task, goal structure, learning activity, positive interdependence,

individual accountability, criteria for success, and collaborative behaviors.

5. Monitor the students, and provide feedback and specific praise regarding the effectiveness of learning groups, and the use of various social skills during group work.

6. Continuously evaluate student achievement related to the specified outcomes of the lessons, and assist students in self-monitoring and in evaluating how well they collaborated.

Two Cooperative Learning Structures

ONE:
Numbered Heads Together

Developed by
Spencer Kagan
Resources for Teachers
27134 Paseo Espada #202
San Juan Capistrano, CA

The purpose of Numbered Heads Together is three-fold: (1) To actively engage all students during teacher led instruction and discussion; (2) To provide a review technique to assess and improve comprehension; and (3) To facilitate collaborative discussion of material.

Steps for implementing Numbered Heads Together:

1. Divide the class into small heterogeneous groups (approximately four to six students per group), carefully considering ability, sex, race, and background.

2. Number the students on each team from 1 to ___.

3. Present the content information to the students. Then ask a question(s) related to the material presented. (Questions can be asked throughout the teacher's presentation or after the presentation.) Ask each team to:
   - Put their Heads Together;
   - Come up with the best answer they can; and
   - Make sure everybody on the team knows the answer.

4. Direct all number _____s who know the answer to raise their hands.

5. Randomly select one student with hand raised to respond.

6. Ask how many other number _____s agree with this answer or how many others can expand upon this answer.

7. Actively recognize and reward correct responses, expansions, and agreements.

8. Administer, score, and record individual quizzes. Publicly post point totals for each learning team on laminated scoreboards.

TWO:
Comprehension Wheels

Developed by
Nancy Livingston
Utah State Office of Education
Modified and adapted by
Susan Fister
Education 1st
1930 Sheridan Road
Salt Lake City, UT 84108

The purpose of Comprehension Wheels is to cultivate social skills, while focusing on improving organizational, listening, comprehension, writing, and study skills.

Steps for implementing Comprehension Wheels:

1. Divide students into small heterogeneous groups of three to five students, assigning a recorder, checker, encourager, and organizer for each group. Define roles and responsibilities and provide modeling of the procedure.

2. Provide each group with scratch paper and one copy of a blank comprehension wheel (provided at the end of this module).

3. Provide students with the story topic, or subject area in which later reading will occur. (For example, "Today you will be reading a selection on dinosaurs.")

4. Instruct all students to formulate and write questions about the topic. This should be a timed brainstorming activity lasting for two or three minutes, using the scratch paper. (All students can write questions, or the recorder can write questions verbalized by each student.)

5. The group organizes the questions into categories such as who, what, when, where, how, how often, why, or characters, details about characters, setting, problem, goal, solutions, etc., eliminating any duplicate or irrelevant questions. The recorder writes each question, one

per spoke, around the wheel, indicating the category of each question. The number of questions generated will determine the total number of spokes around the wheel. This number may vary for each group; however, guidelines or a limit may be set by the teacher.

6. The organizer assigns an equal number of questions to each student. The students' names can be written on the spokes to indicate their assigned questions. Each student is then responsible for gathering information related to his/her question(s) as students independently read (or listen to) the story/passage.

7. The answers/responses are recorded in the space provided on the wheel next to each question. Students check to make sure that all questions have been answered. If answers were not available in the passage, they should discuss and check other references which may contain the necessary information (e.g., encyclopedia, magazines, etc.)

8. Discuss all questions and responses within each learning group. The checker is responsible for making sure that each group member can respond correctly to all questions.

9. The organizer sequences the questions (putting numbers beside each question) in preparation for writing a paragraph about the topic. Time is allowed for each student to develop one or two sentences related to his/her question. The checker makes sure that the sentences are complete and clear.

10. The group develops a beginning sentence and a concluding sentence.

11. The recorder can write the paragraph at the bottom of the wheel, or each student can write his/her sentence(s) in the predetermined sequence.

12. Paragraphs can be traded across learning groups for editing and sharing of information. Points can be assigned for meeting specified criteria such as question format, type of question, sequencing, beginning sentence, concluding sentence, complete sentences, clarity, etc.

13. Schedule time for rewrites if necessary. Provide time at the end of each session for the group to process on roles and teamwork. Team report cards can be completed at the end of each work session. (See illustration at the end of this module.)

14. The teacher can randomly select questions from each wheel from which to develop quizzes. Prior to testing, provide learning groups with study guides containing a list of all questions for practice. Administer quizzes individually and post a total learning group score on a laminated scoreboard for each topic. (See example scoreboard at the end of this module.) Provide rewards for daily or weekly team scores and points for team improvement over subsequent days.

NOTE: The encourager should provide feedback to students throughout the activity, can facilitate completion of the report card, and can tabulate and record points.

These lessons can last several days and are appropriate at both the elementary and secondary level.

Tips and Cautions

1. Begin with short, simple cooperative structures with no more than three to five students in a group/team.

2. Look for opportunities to integrate group work into every subject area, for the purposes of reinforcement, practice, and review of skills and concepts.

3. Clearly model and teach (using examples and non-examples) the concepts of participation and interdependence. If roles are assigned, be sure to teach and practice what is expected of each person.

4. Build in some degree of individual accountability so that all students must prove themselves for evaluative purposes. This way, the unmotivated student will be required to produce something to demonstrate performance. Peer pressure from a group contingency reward structure can also drive the unmotivated student to get involved. It is essential that the teacher carefully monitor the progress of the group to assess each student's input and the dynamics operating within the total group, and to provide ongoing feedback.

5. Provide frequent opportunities for group processing. Questions such as: "What was positive

> Peer pressure from a group contingency reward structure can also drive the unmotivated student to get involved.

about the work?"; "Where is improvement necessary?"; and "What steps should be implemented to achieve these goals?" should be addressed on a regular basis.

6. If students argue or protest about being in a particular group, try: (1) Giving them a strategy for getting work done; (2) Reassessing group composition to make sure there are no "dangerous" combinations of students; (3) Reteaching social skills such as how to disagree appropriately, how to give negative feedback, how to accept criticism, etc.; or (4) Explaining that this is part of the assignment and that this is the way it is for the time being. Group membership can change with the next assignment.

7. Cooperative learning needs to be carefully structured, but it is easy with proper training of students and the necessary preplanning.

References

Johnson, D.W., Maruyama, G., Johnson, R., Nelson, D., & Skon, L. (1981). Effects of cooperative, competitive, and individualistic goal structures on achievement: A meta-analysis. *Psychological Bulletin, 89,* 47-62.

Lovitt, T., Fister, S., Freston, J., Kemp, K., Moore, R.C., & Schroeder, B.E. (1992). *Translating research into practice (TRIP).* Longmont, CO: Sopris West.

Slavin, R.R. (1983). When does cooperative learning increase student achievement? *Psychological Bulletin, 94,* 429-445.

Comprehension Wheel

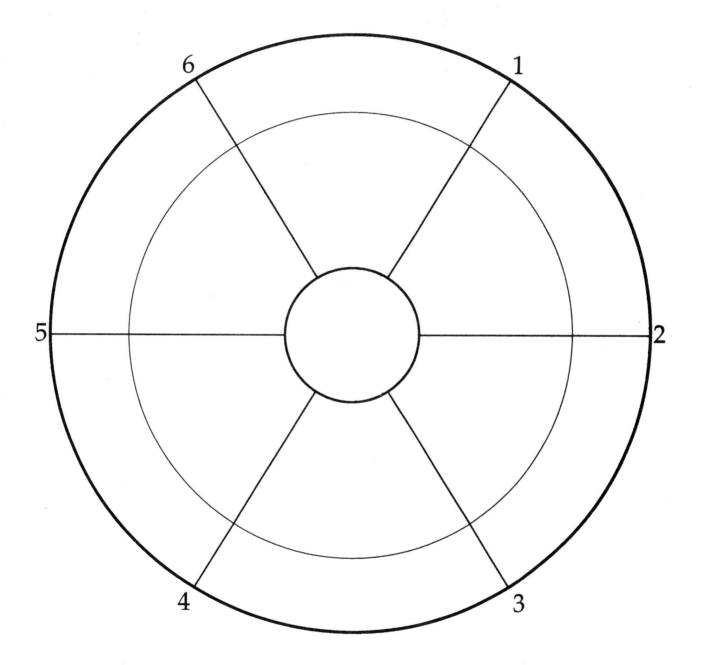

Comprehension Wheel (Key)

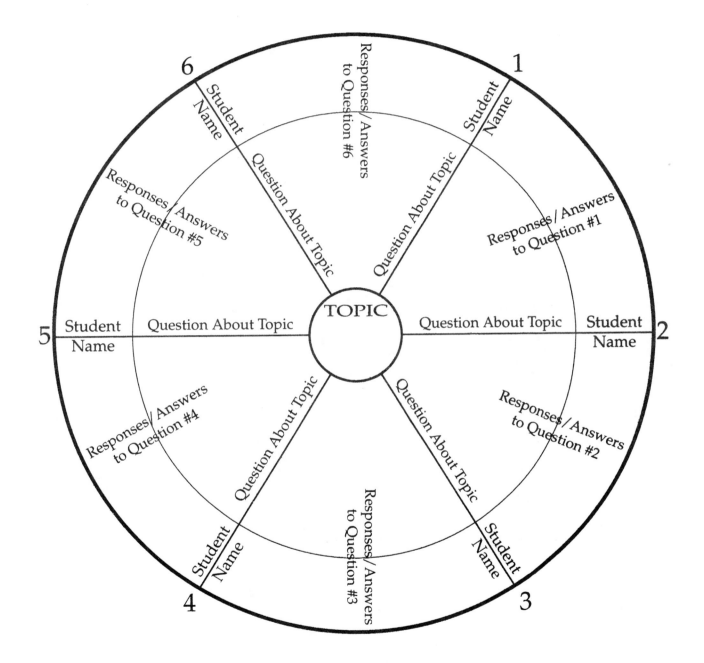

Comprehension Wheel (Sample)

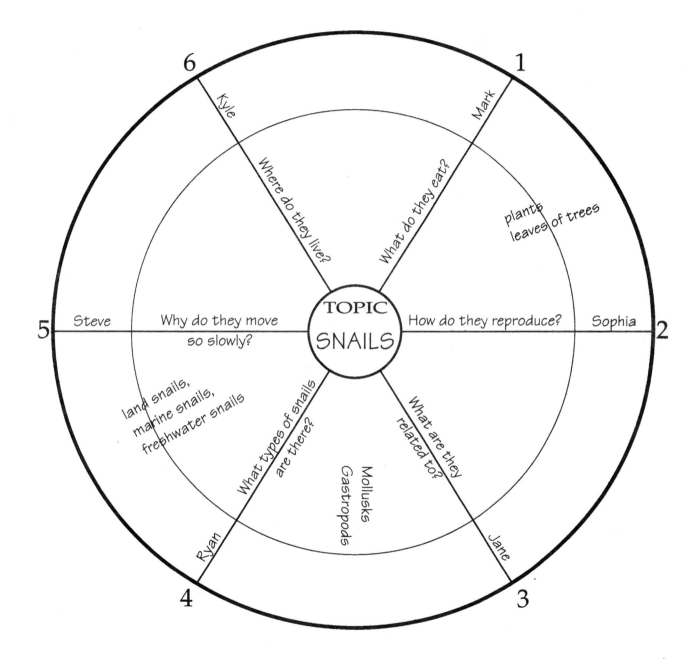

6

1

Kyle

Mark

Where do they live?

What do they eat?

plants
leaves of trees

5 Steve Why do they move
so slowly?

TOPIC

SNAILS

How do they reproduce? Sophia 2

land snails,
marine snails,
freshwater snails

What types of snails
are there?

What are they
related to?

Mollusks
Gastropods

Ryan

Jane

4

3

Team Report Card

For: _____
(TEAM NAME/TOPIC)

1. What skills were we practicing?

2. Names of participants and their roles:

3. What did we accomplish?

4. What was said when we thought someone's idea was good?

5. What was said when we disagreed with someone?

6. Two things we can do to improve how our group works together are:

7. Group grade: **A**   **B**   **C**   **D**

Comprehension Wheel Scoreboard

Team/Group	Topic #1		Topic #2		Topic #3		TOTAL
	Paragraph/ Wheel Points	Quiz Points	Paragraph/ Wheel Points	Quiz Points	Paragraph/ Wheel Points	Quiz Points	
1.							
2.							
3.							
4.							
5.							
6.							

Homenotes to Improve Motivation

by William R. Jenson, Ph.D., University of Utah, and H. Kenton Reavis, Ed.D., Utah State Office of Education

Introduction

A homenote system is one of the most effective techniques for improving a student's motivation and classroom behavior. It is also one of the most mismanaged and underutilized techniques. A homenote system is simply a note, periodically completed by a teacher, that assesses academic and behavioral progress. This note is sent home for the parent(s) to review, apply consequences, and sign, and then is returned to school.

A major strength of a homenote system involves the school-to-home and back-to-school cycle because it informs the parent(s) of their child's progress and allows the use of consequences in the home that are rarely available to the teacher.

Are Homenotes Effective?

There are several published studies and reviews of research about homenote systems that document their effectiveness (Atkeson & Forehand, 1979; Barth, 1979; Broughton, Barton, & Owen, 1981). The available evidence suggests that a well-designed

OBJECTIVES

By the end of this module, you will know:
- The variables that make homenotes effective.
- How to implement a homenote system.
- How to enhance the effectiveness of a homenote system.
- How to solve specific problems associated with homenote systems.

homenote system can improve academic performance and classroom behavior. Academic behaviors that have been improved using a homenote system include listening to the teacher's instructions, participating in class, answering questions, working with eyes and head toward materials, completing classwork neatly, completing homework, and achieving at an appropriate level (Atkeson & Forehand, 1979; Broughton et al., 1981). Specific examples of academic enhancement include improving math scores (Karraker, 1972) and improving in-seat completion of reading assignments from an average of approximately 46% to 84% (Imber, Imber, & Rothstein, 1979).

Many parents are willing and interested in cooperating with teachers.

Classroom behavior also improves with a well-designed homenote system. Frequently, when classroom behaviors improve, there is also an increase in academic performance. Specific classroom behaviors that have been pinpointed for change with homenotes include off-task behavior, aggression, classroom rule violation, tantrums, talkouts, disturbing others, out-of-seat, and other behaviors (Atkeson & Forehand, 1979; Broughton et al., 1981; Barth, 1979; Imber et al., 1979; Taylor, Cornwell, Riley, 1984). All of these behaviors are good candidates for use with homenote systems. One study demonstrated a 90% decrease in disruptive classroom behavior when a homenote program was implemented (Ayllon, Garber, & Pisor, 1975).

What Makes Homenotes Effective?

One important variable is the need to hold a parent meeting or training before a homenote system is implemented. This is designed to orient the parent(s) to the note, help them set up home consequences, and make sure the note is not used in a punitive manner. Training can range from a two-hour training session (Ayllon, et al., 1975) to a telephone parent training session (Imber et al, 1979), or to simply a sheet of instructions that is sent home to the parent(s) and explains the homenote procedures (Lahey, Gendrich, Gendrich, Schnelle, Gant, & McNees, 1977). Face-to-face contact with a parent is the best approach, but whatever method is used, it is important to have some parent contact in which the parent(s) are given directions about receiving, reacting to, and troubleshooting a homenote program.

Other effectiveness variables found in the homenote research literature involve such factors as whether the note is totally positive or contains some type of mild punishment procedure if the student does not perform well or loses the homenote (Atkeson, & Forehand, 1979; Broughton, et al., 1981). Some research indicates that praise for good performance and loss of basic home privileges for poor performance is more effective than just positive consequences (Schumaker, Hovell, & Sherman, 1977).

Other issues include whether a simple yes and no is better than a more detailed rating, whether notes should be sent home daily or only at the end of the week, or the advantages of a simple note as compared to a complex and information-packed note. Each of these issues will be described in the following section.

How to Implement a Homenote System

The basic principles for starting a homenote system are relatively easy and economical. However, several questions should be answered before a homenote system is implemented. First, is there a need? Is a particular student having academic or behavioral difficulties in the classroom? If the answer is yes, then a homenote may be the answer.

Second, are the parent(s) cooperative and willing to start a homenote system? Parents are often willing and are interested in cooperating with teachers. Keep in mind, however, that many parents have been occasionally contacted by school personnel over the years to discuss their child's lack of academic progress or behavioral difficulties. You may be the first teacher to offer cooperation and a solution. So, be patient if the parent(s) are somewhat cautious.

The last question to ask is, am I organized enough as a teacher to start a homenote program? You cannot expect a student to be organized and to perform if you are a model of disorganization. If you forget to sign a homenote, or do not take the time to make appropriate comments, or if you don't make sure the student has a new homenote at the beginning of the week, then you will make a bad impression on the student and parent(s). In addition, if positive consequences are not applied at home for bringing the note home or for good performance, then the student may suffer if you do not follow through. Once you commit to starting a homenote program, you must be organized enough to run it. However, good homenote systems almost run themselves. There are nine basic steps for implementing a homenote program:

STEP ONE

Design a simple note. Complex notes are difficult to complete and they are often not read by parents. If you decide to give a note to a student each day, make sure one note will last for the whole week. It is difficult to photocopy a new note each day. A sample note that can be used with elementary and secondary students can be found at the end of this module. The note has space for five behaviors, and Monday through Friday can be rated on a single sheet of paper.

STEP TWO

Have an idea about which behaviors you would like to list on the note. Again, simplicity is the basic rule. Never have more than five behaviors because it is too difficult for the student to track, and it will be difficult for you to monitor the progress on more than five behaviors. In addition, the homenote should include both academic behaviors and classroom behaviors. For example, a homenote might list: (1) Reading performance, (2) Arithmetic performance, (3) Spelling performance, (4) Paying attention, and (5) Following teacher's directions. This is a good blend of academic and classroom behaviors. The comments section of the note can be used to give the parent(s) additional information or to provide guidelines for homework assignments.

STEP THREE

The next step is to arrange a meeting with the student's parent(s) to discuss the homenote program and to gain their cooperation. Parent contacts can be done on the telephone, through a letter, or by having them come into school for a meeting. If possible, it is best to have the parent(s) come in for a face-to-face meeting. It is also important to remember that many parent(s) have been contacted by the school before. However, many of these contacts have been less than

favorable because their only purpose has been to report about a student's problem without offering help. You should emphasize that you are asking for their input and cooperation, but that you are also going to offer some concrete help. Clearly express your hope that you can work cooperatively together. Once the parent(s) have agreed to the meeting, you should set the following goals:

Goal 1
Ask for the parent(s)' input about what behaviors they would like to see changed.

Goal 2
Describe the behaviors that you would like to list on the homenote. Determine if the parent(s) agree that these are important behaviors (e.g., reading, arithmetic, or spelling performance, paying attention, following teacher's instruction, or being prepared for class).

Goal 3
Determine what positive or mildly aversive consequences the parent(s) can deliver at home depending on the student's performance.

Goal 4:
Ask the parent(s) to read the note each day and make sure it is initialed by you, and to sign it to indicate they have read the note.

Goal 5:
Convince the parent(s) that they should accept no excuse or reason for the student not bringing the note home. Common reasons given by students are: "I lost the note," "There was a substitute teacher who would not fill out the note," "A kid stole the note from me," or "The teacher ran out of notes." In addition, identify a consequence for the student if he/she loses or forgets the note.

Goal 6:
Give the parent(s) a copy of your telephone number so they can call if they are confused about the program or they have a question.

> Once you commit to starting a homenote program, you must be organized enough to run it.

STEP FOUR

It is important to use consequences for homenote performance. There should be positive consequences for appropriate classroom performance and behavior. There should also be mildly aversive consequences for poor performance or classroom misbehavior. Examples of consequences that can be agreed upon in the parent meeting are:

1. For a perfect day, the student stays up 30 minutes later than normal (i.e., if the student's regular bedtime is 8:00 P.M., he/she would stay up until 8:30 P.M.).

2. For each "U" (unsatisfactory) rating, the student goes to bed ten minutes early (i.e., if the student's bedtime is 8:00 P.M., then a note with three "U" marks would mean the student goes to bed at 7:30 P.M.).

3. For a perfect day the student watches an additional 30 minutes of television.

4. For each "U" mark, the student misses 30 minutes of television (i.e., if the student gets two "U" marks, then the student misses one hour from the allotted three hours of television watching).

Other consequences for elementary students might include the right to use a bicycle, time on the Nintendo® video game, computer time, or allowance money earned or lost. For adolescents, consequences might include the right to use the family automobile on the weekend, using the telephone, or listening to music on the family stereo. It is important to find meaningful consequences. Homenotes work if there is something valued that can be earned or lost. However, just earning positive rewards is generally not enough.

STEP FIVE

Decide when the homenote will start and how frequently the note will be given. It is generally better to start off giving the homenote each day and slowly taper off to giving the note only on Fridays, and finally phase the note out altogether. For example, students could be told that when they accumulate eight good or perfect weeks (not necessarily eight weeks in a row), then they will get the note only on Fridays. When they accumulate another eight good weeks, they are off the note entirely.

STEP SIX

Once the first five steps have been performed, you must pick a date on which to start the program. The date should be selected with the parent(s)' input, or at least the parent(s) must be informed. Mondays are the best days to start. It will also help a great deal if the teacher calls the parent(s) at least twice during the first week and once a week for the next two weeks after the program has started. The calls can be used to troubleshoot any problems and to show the parent(s) that you are interested. They also let the student know that there is a firm and cooperative link between you and their parent(s).

STEP SEVEN

On the first day, give the student the note and mark each behavior on it. A general assessment of each behavior is fine. If you are too detailed and take too much time, you are less likely to use the note in the future. Mark the note as accurately as you can, but do not take too much time.

Mark each note with a happy face or frowny face for younger students. For older students or adolescents, a variety of markings can be used: "E" for excellent, "S" for satisfactory, or "U" for unsatisfactory. Other teachers simply mark the note with a plus (+) for satisfactory work or a zero (0) for poor work. Do not use a minus (-) because it can be changed into a plus (+) very easily. It is important also to initial each rating because initials are difficult to forge, and it adds a personal touch that you have marked and reviewed the note.

STEP EIGHT

If possible, make the student successful for the first couple of days with good notes. Some parents are worried that a teacher might use the note to simply punish the student. Making the student successful is important. However, the first time you mark an unsatisfactory behavior on the note, it is good practice to tell the student exactly why he/she is being marked down and then ask the student to repeat the reason (frequently, the parent(s) will ask the student why they got a poor mark and this is a good method to ensure that the student knows the answer). It is also wise, if possible, to call the parent(s) on the day of the poor mark to answer any questions and comment on how well the program is going.

STEP NINE

After the program has been in operation for approximately four to six weeks, arrange another parent conference, or at least make a telephone call to review the student's progress. It is important in this meeting to be optimistic and to emphasize the gains the student has made. This is also an excellent opportunity to troubleshoot any problems in the program.

Troubleshooting a Homenote Program

Problems can occur even with the best programs. Homenotes are particularly prone to problems because they rely on a student to carry the note. However, the problems are fairly easy to fix if you have a well-designed program and a cooperative parent.

PROBLEM: *The student continues to lose the note.*

> **Solution:** Have the student go to bed one hour early, or miss all of television or outside play time each day he/she forgets the note. It is important to emphasize to the student that no excuses are accepted and that it is his/her responsibility to ask the teacher for the note at the end of the school day.

PROBLEM: *The student changes the ratings or forges your initials.*

> **Solution:** Changing a rating (i.e., making a sad face happy) or forging initials should be handled like a lost note. No excuses should be accepted and the student should go to bed an hour early or lose all television privileges. It is important to prepare the parent(s) for this problem. It is not uncommon, particularly if a student may lose some of his/her privileges because of poor ratings from the teacher. The parent(s) should have your telephone number to call if they suspect that the homenote has been altered.

A frequent excuse used by students is that they marked the note because their teacher was absent and the substitute teacher did not know how to mark it. In such instances,

Homenotes are particularly prone to problems because they rely on a student to carry the note. However, the problems are fairly easy to fix if you have a well-designed program and a cooperative parent.

the student should be taught to ask someone in the principal's office for help with the note if the substitute teacher is unaware of the procedures. This person (a secretary or aide) could go with the student and ask the substitute for the rating, answering any questions that the substitute might have.

PROBLEM: *The student refuses to take the note.*

> **Solution:** This is a relatively rare problem, but it does occur. If the student flatly refuses to take the note, have the parent(s) consistently implement the procedures for a lost note (i.e., to bed early, no television, or loss of outside play privileges). It may be important to be a support for the parent(s) during this difficult time. A telephone call and confident reassurance can help a great deal. Most children and adolescents will come around in about a week after the parent(s) have consistently applied the consequences. However, it may help to enhance the program by using some type of reinforcement procedure in the classroom for the student taking and using the note. Several reinforcement procedures will be discussed in the next section.

PROBLEM: *The parent(s) are willing to look at the note, but they have difficulty applying consequences at home for the program.*

> **Solution #1:** Try putting together a reinforcer kit and delivering it to the home. The kit can contain some simple reinforcers (e.g., candy, stickers, little toys) that the parent(s) can give the student for a good note.

> **Solution #2:** Obtain the parent(s)' permission to apply the consequences for the note in your classroom. At least have the parent(s) review and sign the note. When it is returned the next day, then you can manage some in-class reinforcers (e.g., mystery motivator, spinner, grab bag) or mild punishers (e.g., missing recess, having to stay after school, eating lunch in the classroom and not in the lunchroom, no in-class free time).

PROBLEM *You suspect that the parent(s) may be abusive to the student if he/she receives a poor note.*

> **Solution:** This is a serious problem, but it occurs rarely. If you have reason to suspect it, you should ask the parent(s) to come in, and ask for their cooperation in helping to apply the agreed-upon consequences (both positive and mildly aversive). Tell them that if they punish too much it will make the program fail and the student will learn to dislike school. Then, if you suspect that abuse is still occurring, you may have to discontinue the program (or notify the appropriate authorities if the abuse is severe).

PROBLEM: *A parent refuses to participate in the program and will not even sign the note.*

> **Solution:** Ask the parent(s) for a face-to-face meeting. In the meeting ask about their concerns, and determine if you can answer any of the difficult ones they may have. If both parents come in, appeal to the parent who seems more willing to participate. Explain that the homenote program is not designed to punish the student, but to give the student feedback about his/her performance and to keep the parent(s) informed. Ask if they would be willing to try the program for as little as two weeks. If the parent(s) still refuse, tell them that you would like to give the student the note anyway and you hope they will look at the note (in this case make sure the note is primarily positive for the first week).

Enhancing Homenote Performance Techniques

Homenotes work well if they are designed as described previously. However, it sometimes helps to add some techniques that will make an unmotivated student work even harder or overcome some of the problems associated with homenotes. Some of these techniques are:

1. **Unique Reinforcers:** Reinforcers can be classroom-based or home-based. Their general function is to motivate the students to do well with their note ratings and to bring the note home and back to school. An example of a unique reinforcer is a refrigerator mystery

motivator. The mystery motivator is simply an sealed envelope that is placed on the refrigerator.

Inside the envelope is a slip of paper that has a reward written on it. Once or twice a week, if the student brings the note home with all good markings, the student then gets the mystery motivator. It may help if the teacher calls the parent(s) to tell them it is a mystery motivator day or writes on the homenote a prearranged code for the parent that indicates it is a mystery motivator day.

Another unique reinforcement system that works equally well is a spinner. If the student brings the note home with all good markings, he/she is allowed to spin the arrow. Whatever the arrow lands on, the student gets.

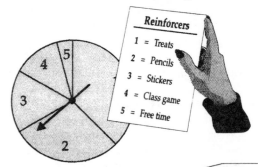

Another program is a grab bag that has five or six rewards in it. The student is allowed to select one reward without looking on days of good homenote performance.

Unique reinforcement systems can be used either at home (as in these examples) or in the classroom if the student does well. However, these are added incentives and should not take the place of the basic privileges and mild punishers that have already been discussed.

2. **Random Notes:** Some teachers would like to use a homenote system with their whole class; however, the time involved in completing 20 to 30 notes is prohibitive. One approach that has shown excellent results is to pick two or three students randomly at the end of each day and send notes home with them. This approach was used by Saudergras, Madsen, and Scott (1977). They compared the effects of sending a note home on Fridays only (fixed) as opposed to sending it home with randomly selected students

on any day of the week (variable). The fixed notes produced an 80% total assigned academic work completed. The random approach increased work production to 140%. Clearly, a random note approach with a whole class is an effective technique.

If two or three students are picked at random in a class each day to take a note home, it helps to tell the students that you will call one of their parents to talk about the note and make sure that it got home.

3. **Group Contingencies:** Group contingencies provide a consequence to a group depending on the behavior of one or two students. Gresham (1983) used a group contingency in combination with a homenote to improve the classroom behavior of an eight-year old mildly retarded male, Billy. Billy had an extreme history of destructive behavior in his foster home that included setting fires, destroying property, and aggression toward his foster siblings. The foster mother requested help from the teacher and school psychologist, and a homenote program was implemented. If Billy's home behavior was nondestructive, he earned juice time, recess, tokens, and a Billy party for the whole class on Friday. The use of a group contingency reduced Billy's destructive acts from an average of three per day to virtually zero per day.

4. **Homenotes as a Behavioral Contract:** Sometimes it is useful to use the homenote program in conjunction with a classroom behavioral contract. For example, have students save their 100% week homenotes. These are the perfect homenotes in which the student has earned all positive ratings for the whole week. Each 100% homenote is worth a ticket. When a student has saved enough tickets, he/she receives a special reward or privilege. The student might have to save four 100% homenotes and then receive a special treat—being taken by the teacher to a fast food restaurant for lunch. Behavioral contracts can also be combined with a group contingency. When a student earns four 100% homenotes, then the entire class is allowed to watch a special video and have a popcorn party.

Do not set the requirement so that the student has to earn a set number of notes in a row. Instead, make the requirement cumulative so that students can save all their 100% notes, even if they have poor weeks in between. A cumulative requirement is much better than a stringent consecutive requirement.

Cautions

Some teachers object to the use of homenotes. The most common objections include:

1. "Homenotes take too much time to fill out." A well-designed homenote takes approximately 30 to 60 seconds to fill out.

2. "Parents will not take the time to read the note and do the program." The research clearly shows that a majority of parents approve of the homenote program and will work with teachers.

3. "Students will lose the notes or counterfeit the signatures." This sometimes happens, but a well-designed homenote program has built-in safeguards to stop these problems.

4. "Homenotes are only effective in the beginning and lose their effectiveness as the program continues." This proves not to be true when the research is reviewed. A well-designed homenote system can produce durable changes in motivation and behavior.

5. "Homenotes are only effective with younger students, not secondary students." This is not true; much of the application research has been done with secondary students.

Case Study

Jake is a ten-year old student in the fifth grade who has been having both academic and behavioral difficulties over the past two years. Jake's mother approached the teacher and asked if there was any type of extra help or counseling that might help Jake and get him back on the right path. She explained that she was a single mother and had some difficulty supervising Jake while she was at work each day. When she was home, she could manage Jake, and she usually tried to get information from him about how well he did that day in school and about his homework assignments. Jake indicated that he was doing very well, and that he did his homework at school, neither of which was true. The mother appeared concerned and responsible and tried to provide a structured home life for Jake. She had him do a set of chores each day, and had a set bedtime of 9:00 P.M. for Jake and his younger brother.

The teacher immediately recognized the advantages in this case. First, the mother had approached the teacher for help and appeared very cooperative. Second, although Jake was unsupervised until the mother got home, she could then manage his behavior. Third, the mother wanted daily information about Jake's progress in the class and his homework assignments. Fourth, Jake had shown an interest in whatever rewards and reinforcers the teacher had used in the classroom. Fifth, when the teacher interviewed the mother about home practices, the mother indicated that Jake did not like his bedtime of 9:00 P.M. and preferred to stay up later with the mother watching television.

The mother and teacher decided to implement a homenote program starting the following Monday, and they exchanged telephone numbers in case there were questions or difficulties. The consequences were: (1) Jake was allowed to stay up an additional 30 minutes past his 9.00 P.M. bedtime for a perfect homenote, (2) For each zero on his homenote Jake went to bed ten minutes early, and (3) When Jake accumulated three perfect weeks (not necessarily in a row) of homenotes he could cash them in for lunch with the teacher. If Jake lost the homenote or altered the ratings, he went to bed one hour early (8:00 P.M.) and lost his television privileges the next day. In addition, the teacher implemented an in-class mystery motivator. She wrote a reward (e.g., getting to sit anywhere in class, ten minutes free time with a buddy, candy from the class store, etc.) on a piece of paper and put it in an envelope. She wrote on the outside of the envelope a day of the week, and did not show it to Jake. If he brought his note back to class signed by his mother that day, he would receive the mystery motivator. Jake could receive from one to two mystery motivators each week.

It was explained to Jake that it was his responsibility to deliver the note to the teacher at the end of the day and have it signed. The teacher and parent would accept no excuses. The behaviors on the note included: (1) Acceptable work in reading, (2) Acceptable work in arithmetic, (3) Completing and turning in the daily assigned homework, (4) Paying attention in class, and (5) No arguing behavior. Jake was

also required to write his daily homework assignment on the Comments section of the note. Each day the teacher would initial the note, and at home when the mother read the note, she would initial it also.

As predicted, the first week went fairly well and the teacher made sure that Jake was successful and that he earned two mystery motivators. However, on the second week, Jake had difficulties and lost the note. He simply indicated to his mother that the teacher forgot to make up a new note and would give him one tomorrow. The mother called the teacher, and Jake went to bed an hour early and he lost television privileges the next day. Jake was irate the next day in class and tore up the note and said he would not participate. He was particularly angry because his younger brother was allowed to stay up and watch television when Jake had to go to bed an hour early. The teacher called the mother at work and discussed the problem. They both decided they could wait longer than Jake. That night he again went to bed an hour early and lost the next day's television privileges. He threw a temper tantrum and stomped out of the house, but came back and was put in bed by his mother. The next day he asked for the note, and did exceptionally well in class. The program has been running for two months. Jake has won three teacher contracts, received the mystery motivator eight times, and is doing particularly well in class. He could be taken off the program; however, the mother wants to continue because it gives her the basic information she needs in order to track Jake's school progress.

References

Ayllon, T., Garber, S., & Pisor, K. (1975). The elimination of discipline problems through a combined school-home motivational system. *Behavior Therapy*, 6(5), 616-626.

Atkeson, B. & Forehand, R. (1979). Home-based reinforcement programs designed to modify classroom behavior: A review and methodological evaluation. *Psychological Bulletin*, 86(6), 1298-1308.

Barth, J. (1979). A review of neuromuscular reeducation: A neurological biofeedback perspective. *American Journal of Clinical Biofeedback*, 2(1), 32-33.

Broughton, S., Barton, E.S., & Owen, P.R. (1981). Home-based contingency systems for school problems. *School Psychology Review, 10*(1), 26-36.

Gresham, F.M. (1983). Use of a home-based dependent group contingency system in controlling destructive behavior: A case study. *School Psychology Review, 12*(2), 195-199.

Imber, S., Imber, R., & Rothstein C. (1979). Modifying independent work habits: An effective teacher-parent communication program. *Exceptional Children, 46*(1), 218-221.

Karraker, R.J. (1972). Disadvantaged adolescents and delay of reinforcement in a token economy. *Proceedings of the Annual Convention of American Psychological Association, 7*(2), 763-764.

Lahey, B.B., Gendrich, J.G., Gendrich, S.I., Schnelle, J.F., Gant, D.S., & McNees, M.P. (1977). An evaluation of report cards with minimal teacher and parent contacts as an efficient method of classroom intervention. *Behavior Modification, 1*(3), 381-384.

Saudergras, R.W., Madsen, C.H., & Scott, J.W. (1977). Differential effects of fixed and variable time feedback on production rates of elementary school children. *Journal of Applied Behavior Analysis, 10*(4), 673-678.

Schumaker, J.B., Hovell, M.F., & Sherman, J.A. (1977). An analysis of daily report cards and parent-managed privileges in the improvement of adolescent classroom performance. *Journal of Applied Behavior Analysis, 10*(3), 449-464.

Taylor, V.L., Cornwell, D.D., & Riley, M.T. (1984). Home-based contingency management programs that teachers can use. *Psychology in the Schools, 21*(3), 368-374.

My Daily Homenote

Name: _____   Month of: _____

Behavior(s) or Subject(s)	Mon.		Tues.		Wed.		Thurs.		Fri.	
	Rating	Teacher Initials	Rating	Teacher Initials	Rating	Teacher Initials	Rating	Teacher Initials	Rating	Teacher Initials

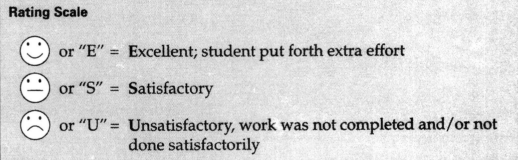

Rating Scale

☺ or "E" = Excellent; student put forth extra effort

😐 or "S" = Satisfactory

☹ or "U" = Unsatisfactory, work was not completed and/or not done satisfactorily

Comments:

Monday _____

Tuesday _____

Wednesday _____

Thursday _____

Friday _____

Using Overcorrection to Improve Academic Performance

by William R. Jenson, Ph.D., University of Utah, and H. Kenton Reavis, Ed.D., Utah State Office of Education

Introduction

Overcorrection is an educational technique that teachers have used for quite some time. Overcorrection means repeating a behavior, the correct way, until it is literally over-corrected, that is exaggerated. Teachers use this technique in several ways. For example, if a student teases another student, the teacher might have the student write, "I am sorry, I will not tease in the future," 100 times on the blackboard. Similarly, if students are running down the halls, a teacher might have them walk down the hall

OBJECTIVES

By the end of this module, you will know:

- The definition of positive practice overcorrection and restitutional overcorrection.
- How to implement overcorrection procedures for academic problems.
- Specific applications of overcorrection procedures to spelling, oral reading, math, and word reversal problems.
- How to solve specific problems that may arise when using overcorrection procedures.
- Cautions when using overcorrection procedures.

ten times. In both of these examples, a misbehavior is consequated by practicing the correct behavior. In the teasing example, the student repeatedly practices writing an apology and a promise. In the running example, the students repeatedly practice walking down the halls correctly.

There is a great deal of research supporting the effectiveness of overcorrection. For instance, overcorrection procedures have been used to improve attention problems, aggression, sharing problems, toileting accidents, vandalism, swearing, and many other inappropriate behaviors. The authors have used it for their own children for failing to pick up dishes (pick them up ten times), leaving doors open (shut door ten times), or dropping clothes or toys on the floor (pick them up ten times). This type of overcorrection is called **positive practice** because the child has to practice the correct behavior numerous times.

Positive practice overcorrection can also be used with academic problems because of its drill and practice features. Many students are unmotivated because they have not mastered an essential skill that is needed before the next academic skill can be taught. As skill deficits increase, the student becomes less and less motivated. The drill and practice component of positive practice overcorrection helps a student acquire and master the skill. It is particularly useful for spelling, mathematics facts, reading and writing skills that require practice for mastery.

> Overcorrection works best where practice is needed to master a skill such as writing letters, letter reversal correction, spelling, sight words, oral reading, or math facts.

A second type of overcorrection is called **restitutional overcorrection**. This type of overcorrection has less application to academic skills than it has for classroom misbehavior. With restitutional overcorrection, a student is required to make the environment better than it was before the misbehavior occurred. For example, if a student spits on another student's desk, the spitter would be required to clean the tops of all the desks in the room. Similarly, if a student threatens another student, he/she would be required to apologize to everyone in the classroom. In some instances, restitutional overcorrection may require manual guidance of the student until the student starts the appropriate behavior. Restitutional overcorrection has limited application for increasing academic motivation.

General Steps for Implementing an Overcorrection Procedure

STEP ONE:

Decide what academic skill the student needs. Overcorrection works best where practice is needed to master a skill such as writing letters, letter reversal correction, spelling, sight words, oral reading, or math facts.

STEP TWO

Design a worksheet that a student can use to practice the academic operation. It helps if the worksheet is lined and numbered. Numbering helps a student keep track of the number of repetitions needed.

STEP THREE

Set up a time each day when he/she independently practices the skill at his or her desk. Independent practice works well with spelling, mathematics, and writing. It is more difficult with reading skills.

STEP FOUR

It is easy to forget about a student when he/she is engaged in independent overcorrection practice. It is critical that teachers circulate around the classroom and verbally praise students who are on-task and working. Younger students respond to overt verbal praise and a touch. Older students are less responsive to verbal praise and may respond better to quiet praise and a touch on the shoulder.

STEP FIVE

A parallel reinforcement system is always needed when working with overcorrection for unmotivated students. Reinforcement systems that are random and that pay off frequently at the start are best. Several suggestions for reinforcement systems are:

1. Random, on-task "beep tape" or timer with points as reinforcement for attending and working.

2. Mystery motivators, spinners, and grab bags can be used with individual students or with an entire group.

3. Contracts can be used, with worksheets being saved up to meet a cumulative criterion. Contracts should not be the only reinforcement system used with overcorrection; they work best as an adjunct to the basic point system suggested in item 1.

4. Magic pens are effective. One pen in the set is filled with invisible ink; the other pens are used to make the invisible ink visible. A box is placed in the upper right hand corner of each worksheet. Some of the boxes have an invisible star in them. When students finish a worksheet, they color the box to see if the star appears. If there is a star, the student receives a mystery motivator. When the student starts the overcorrection practice, the first three sheets have stars, then approximately every other sheet, and, finally, every third sheet or so has a star.

STEP SIX

It helps if a student's progress is plotted and publicly posted in the classroom. Public posting can be used in conjunction with a behavioral contract.

Specific Applications of Overcorrection Procedures

Spelling

Three studies have demonstrated the effectiveness of positive practice overcorrection for spelling (Foxx & Jones, 1978; Ollendick, Matson, Esveldt-Dawson, & Shapiro, 1980; Stewart & Singh, 1986). The participants were students who were classified mentally retarded and emotionally disturbed. Two basic strategies have been used in these studies:

Pronunciation Method

1. Teacher pronounces the word.
2. Student pronounces the word.
3. Student pronounces the letters as the word is spelled by teacher.
4. Correct spelling is praised by teacher.
5. For misspelled words, student is required to write the word five times, saying each letter

aloud. (This is the most important part of this procedure.)

Dictionary Method

Student is given a spelling pretest. For each misspelled word, the student:

1. Writes the word correctly, using a dictionary or spelling book.
2. Also writes the word's correct phonetic spelling.
3. Writes the word as part of speech.
4. Writes the word's complete dictionary definition.
5. Uses the word correctly in five sentences other than the sentences in the dictionary or spelling book.

Both of these approaches were very effective in improving spelling skills. Social validity ratings from the students indicated that most students liked the procedures. The main disadvantage to the Pronunciation Method is the teacher's one-on-one instructional time. This procedure could be modified for independent work. The disadvantages for the Dictionary Method are the requirements for the student to write complete sentences and to use a dictionary.

Oral Reading Skills

Two studies have examined the effects of positive practice overcorrection procedures with oral reading skills (Singh & Singh, 1986; Singh, Singh, & Winton, 1984). Again, two basic methods have been used:

The Drill Method

Here are the teacher instructions for the Drill Method:

> "Here is a story. I want you to read it. I will help you if you make any mistakes. I will tell you the correct word and then you can go on reading. After you have completed your reading, I will print on cards all the words you did not read correctly and we will go over them until you can read them correctly. Try your best not to make any mistakes."

1. The student reads a selected passage.
2. Errors are noted by the teacher and the correct word is given.

3. At the end of the passage, the teacher makes flash cards for all the incorrectly read words.

4. The student is drilled on the flash cards with corrective feedback until achieving 100% accuracy.

Positive Practice-Repeat Method

Here are the teacher instructions for the Positive Practice-Repeat Method:

"Here is a story. I want you to read it. I will help you if you make mistakes. I will tell you the correct word while you listen and point to the word in the book. After that, I want you to point to and say the word five times. Then you will read the sentence again. Try your best not to make any mistakes, but if you do make one and correct yourself, I will give you lots of praise for doing so."

1. Student reads a short passage.

2. When the student makes an oral reading mistake, the correct word is pronounced by the teacher while the student points at the word in the passage.

3. Then the student points to the word and says it five times.

4. The student then reads the complete sentence again that contained the word.

The Drill Method is about twice as effective in reducing oral reading errors as doing nothing (e.g., letting the student read with corrective feedback from the teacher, but not requiring the student to correct the error). However, the Positive Practice-Repeat Method is twice as effective as the Drill Method in reducing oral errors. It is important when using these procedures to consider pauses (ten to 15 seconds) and omissions as errors. Reinforcing the student verbally or with edibles for self-corrections (i.e., no teacher assistance in correcting the error) increased self-corrections and reduced overall errors.

A disadvantage of both methods is that they require one-to-one teacher instructional time. The Drill Method also has the disadvantage of requiring a teacher to make flash cards immediately after a passage is read. However, parent tutoring or peer tutoring might reduce the overall one-to-one teacher

> Overcorrection procedures work best on math facts that require memorization. Simple addition, subtraction, and multiplication facts can be learned with overcorrection procedures.

instruction time required. A disadvantage of the Positive Practice-Repeat Method is that repeating a word five times disturbs the basic flow of reading the passage.

Math Practice

Overcorrection procedures work best on math facts that require memorization, such as simple addition, subtraction, and multiplication facts. An effective overcorrection procedure is the Cover, Copy, and Compare Method (Skinner, Turco, Beaty, & Resavage, 1989).

Cover, Copy, and Compare Method

1. A list of math facts is developed (see three separate lists for multiplication, following). These facts are listed on the left side of the Data Sheet (see sample at the end of this module).

2. The student looks at the first problem and its solution (e.g., $2 \times 3 = 6$).

3. The problem is covered with an index card.

4. The student writes the problem with its solution to the right of the covered problem.

5. The problem is uncovered and compared with what the student has written.

6. If an error is made, the student repeats the process with the same problem.

7. If the problem is correct, the student moves on to the next problem.

8. The student completes three separate sheets of problems (lists that have the same problems but in a different order) at each session. This ensures the student has correct practice with each problem at least three times.

Examples of Math Problems

List A	List B	List C
$2 \times 6 = 12$	$2 \times 9 = 18$	$2 \times 5 = 10$
$2 \times 7 = 14$	$3 \times 6 = 18$	$3 \times 4 = 12$
$3 \times 5 = 15$	$3 \times 7 = 21$	$3 \times 9 = 27$
$3 \times 8 = 24$	$4 \times 4 = 16$	$4 \times 7 = 28$
$4 \times 6 = 24$	$4 \times 5 = 20$	$5 \times 5 = 25$
$4 \times 9 = 36$	$4 \times 8 = 32$	$5 \times 7 = 35$
$5 \times 6 = 30$	$5 \times 8 = 40$	$6 \times 6 = 36$
$5 \times 9 = 45$	$6 \times 7 = 42$	$6 \times 8 = 48$
$7 \times 7 = 49$	$7 \times 9 = 63$	$6 \times 9 = 54$
$8 \times 9 = 72$	$9 \times 9 = 81$	$7 \times 8 = 56$

An advantage of a Cover, Copy, and Compare overcorrection procedure is that it can be done independently by the student with periodic checking by the teacher. It also gives the student frequent practice with each math problem. The basic disadvantage of the system is that it can be boring and, thus, needs some type of reinforcement system for completing the problems. Suggestions for reinforcement systems will be discussed following.

Letter Reversals

Much has been written about the significance of reversing alphabetic letters such as "b" and "d." Reversals are common before age seven. Most reversals can be reviewed as a discrimination problem. Similar letters such as a "b" and "d" are confused because they look alike. Similar words may also be confused such as saw and was. The best way to learn not to make reversal errors is to practice. Overcorrection is an excellent practice method.

Cover, Copy, and Compare Method

The method is Cover, Copy, and Compare and is essentially the same as for math facts with these exceptions:

1. The student should say the letter from a list.
2. The student should trace the letter as it is said.
3. The letter should be covered with an index card.
4. The letter should be copied three to five times to the right of the covered letter. Each time the letter is copied, it should be compared to the covered letter on the list and said aloud.
5. Errors should be immediately corrected by a teacher (or aide, or peer tutor) and the student required to write the correct letter.
6. Lists of random letters (or words) should be developed (i.e., "d, b, p, q, r, t, m, g, p, l, t" or "was, saw, as, cat, tac, saw, the, was").
7. If the problem is correct, the student moves on to the next problem.

Troubleshooting an Overcorrection Program

PROBLEM: _The student refuses to do the procedure. This is because it is boring to repeat a task that you perform poorly. It is the most common problem._

Solution: Re-think the motivation system you are using. Try using a Mystery Motivator, change the types of rewards you use, use a public posting system for progress, or combine with a homenote system. Be sure to verbally praise the student even for small increases in performance.

PROBLEM: _The student has difficulty getting started or takes too long to complete the overcorrection practice._

Solution: Use a "beat the buzzer" approach. Make a bonus reward dependent on the student finishing before a timer goes off. Make sure that you give the student enough time to finish but not so much time that it can be wasted with off-task behaviors.

PROBLEM: _The student is not making adequate progress even though the overcorrection practice sessions are being completed._

Solution: Check to make sure that the student is not making errors and then practicing them in the overcorrection procedure. This can be disastrous. The only way to prevent errors is to monitor the student closely. If monitoring reveals that errors are still occurring, then the student may need more practice. Include one more overcorrection session with a bonus reward.

PROBLEM: _The student is off-task or seems to be daydreaming when he should be doing the overcorrection procedure._

Solution: There are two approaches to improving on-task behavior. First, try a random "beep tape" with points for on-task behavior. Second, check the pacing of the presentation of the material. If the practice items to be given to the student require a presentation by a teacher, then increasing the pace of presentation may increase performance.

PROBLEM: _The student tantrums or becomes frustrated with the overcorrection procedure._

Solution: First, check your motivation program. Has the student received a reward recently? If not, rig the system for an immediate payoff. Second, the number of items required to practice may be too many or take too much time. Break the task into two sessions. Or, give the student a break. Or, contract for completion of the task without a tantrum. Be careful not to reduce the task too much because tantrums can be a manipulation to avoid work. It is better to break the session in half than to reduce the number of response opportunities. There is no substitute for practice.

Cautions

Caution is needed when using overcorrection as an academic enhancement technique. Technically, overcorrection is defined as a punishment technique. Punishment techniques are used to suppress or reduce a behavior. Overcorrection is one of the only punishment techniques in which the student learns something useful while engaging in the behavior. If used alone, positive practice overcorrection would be a punishing experience for the student, who would eventually not want to participate. To obtain the benefits of overcorrection with academic subjects, the technique must be paired with some type of unique motivating reward or contract. The positive consequence is the key to motivating students to engage in the overcorrection technique.

Case Study

Tim is a first grade student who has had a great deal of difficulty learning to print his letters. Some professionals have suggested that he needs an extensive evaluation of his writing difficulties. Specifically, Tim has a terrible time with the letters "b" and "d." However, his teacher is convinced that he can learn letter discriminations if he is given enough opportunity. She has set up an extra work program for Tim to practice in which he is reinforced for writing repeated "b"s and "d"s.

The teacher has dictated on five cassettes the following: "Trial One—write b" or "Trial Two—write d" for a total of 50 trials. Each cassette has a different or random list of "b"s and "d"s (25 each). Tim sits at a work station with a tape player, cassette, two 3 x 5 cards (one with a "b" printed along with a picture of the insect bee and one with a "d" and a picture of a duck) and a lined worksheet that is numbered one through fifty.

The 3 x 5 cards are placed face down on the desk. Tim plays the first trial from the cassette and writes the dictated letter. He then turns over one of the 3 x 5 cards and compares his written letter with the sample on the card. If he is correct, he goes on to the next trial. If he is wrong, he writes the letter five times correctly with the 3 x 5 card as an example. At the end of the session, he is allowed to spin a spinner for a reinforcer.

Tim has made significant progress in reducing the number of reversal errors. Although he has been at 100% correct for several days, the teacher continues to have him practice so that the skill is overlearned.

References

Foxx, R.M. & Jones, J.R. (1978). A remediation program for increasing the spelling achievement of elementary and junior high school students. *Behavior Modification, 2*(2), 211-230.

Ollendick, T.H., Matson, J.L., Esveldt-Dawson, K., & Shapiro, E.S. (1980). Increasing spelling achievement: An analysis of treatment procedures utilizing an alternative treatments design. *Journal of Applied Behavior Analysis, 13*(4), 645-654.

Singh, N.N. & Singh, J. (1986). A behavioral remediation program for oral reading: Effects on errors and comprehension. *Educational Psychology, 6*(2), 105-114.

Singh, N.N., Singh, J., & Winton, A.S. (1984). Positive practice overcorrection of oral reading errors. *Behavior Modification, 8*(1), 23-27.

Skinner, C.H., Turco, T.L., Beatty, K.L., & Rasavage, C. (1989). Cover, copy, and compare: A method for increasing multiplication performance. *School Psychology Review, 18*(3), 412-420.

Stewart, C.A. & Singh, N.N. (1986). Overcorrection of spelling deficits in moderately mentally retarded children. *Behavior Modification, 10*(3), 355-365.

Cover, Copy, and Compare Method
Data Sheet

First Answer   Practice Repetitions

1. _____   _____
2. _____   _____
3. _____   _____
4. _____   _____
5. _____   _____
6. _____   _____
7. _____   _____
8. _____   _____
9. _____   _____
10. _____   _____
11 _____   _____
12. _____   _____
13. _____   _____
14. _____   _____
15. _____   _____
16. _____   _____
17. _____   _____
18. _____   _____
19. _____   _____
20. _____   _____
21. _____   _____
22. _____   _____

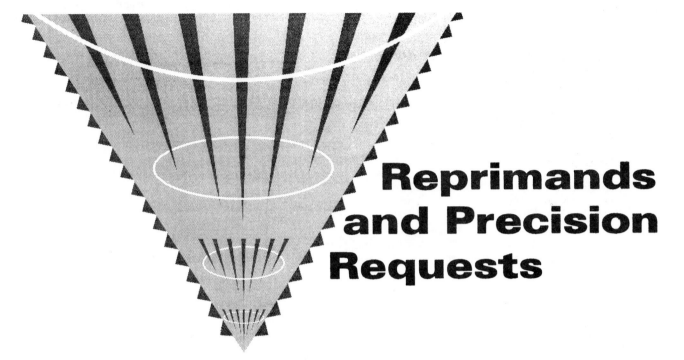

Reprimands and Precision Requests

by William R. Jenson, Ph.D., University of Utah, and H. Kenton Reavis, Ed.D., Utah State Office of Education

Introduction

Reprimands are the most common form of punishment used by teachers and parents. A reprimand is defined as a gestural or verbal rebuke of a behavior. The majority of reprimands are used by persons in authority (i.e., parents and teachers) to stop or reduce a child's misbehavior. However, they can sometimes be used to increase a behavior (e.g., "Now get to work"). In addition, many reprimands carry the threat of a consequence if a student does not comply. However, most reprimands are generally made before an actual consequence is delivered. Reprimands are different from precision requests, which will be discussed in detail later in this module.

The average elementary or junior high school teacher uses some type of verbal reprimand every two minutes (White, 1975), while high school teach-

ers reprimand only about half as often. Interestingly, teacher reprimands exceed teacher praise in every grade after the second. Teachers also use significantly more reprimands with low-ability students when compared to their rates with higher-ability

OBJECTIVES

By the end of this module, you will know:

- The difference between a reprimand and a precision request.
- The variables that make reprimands and precision requests effective.
- How to issue a reprimand or precision request.
- How to solve problems that may arise with reprimands or precision requests.

students (Heller & White, 1975). This means that students of lower ability or motivation may find school less and less rewarding the higher their grade level, because they are reprimanded more and receive less praise.

A recent survey also indicates that teachers still prefer reprimands as their primary motivation and discipline technique (based on a survey of 1,800 teachers reported in _US Today_ in 1988).

Percentage of Teachers Surveyed Who Often Use:	
Oral reprimand	41.9%
Call parent	21.7%
Revoke privileges	17.3%
Detention	10.0%
Isolate from class	6.1%
Send to principal	2.0%
Corporal punishment	0.3%

Thus, reprimands are a fact of educational life that teachers will no doubt continue to use.

Are Reprimands Effective?

The answer to this question is yes. Reprimands can be very effective if they are used properly. However, their effectiveness is temporary and only a short-term solution. To make reprimands effective over the long term, they must not be over-used and should also be combined with other classroom management techniques (Van Houten & Doley, 1983).

Behavior

Reprimands can be helpful in reducing disruptive behavior in a classroom. For example, in one study, two disruptive fifth graders, John and Russell, were reprimanded by a teacher for their classroom misbehavior (Van Houten, Nau, MacKenzie-Keating, Sameoto, & Calavecchia, 1982). The boys were disruptive approximately 60% of the time in their mathematics class. When the teacher effectively reprimanded John, Russell's behavior immediately improved even though Russell's behavior was not reprimanded. Similarly, when Russell's behavior was reprimanded, John's behavior spontaneously improved. Clearly, classroom behavior can be improved temporarily when reprimands are used effectively.

Academics

Can reprimands improve academic motivation? This is a more difficult question. However, there is some evidence to show that effective reprimands can also improve academic skills. In the same study described previously, an analysis was made of Russell's and John's academic performance in their math class. Before the teacher used reprimands for classroom misbehavior, academic performance was poor. On average, Russell completed about 15% of his assignments and John completed about 20%. When reprimands were used with John for his misbehavior, his academic production shot up to 60%. Interestingly, Russell's academic production also increased dramatically to 80%, even when the reprimands were not directed toward him. This is another example of the "spill-over effect" with the use of effective reprimands. The behavior and academic performance of students seated near the reprimanded student may improve.

However, it is important to point out that the reprimands used in this study were used effectively. That is, the teacher's positive reinforcement rate was high, and several other important variables were in place.

What Makes Reprimands Effective?

There are several variables that influence the effectiveness of reprimands. First, reprimands should not be over-used. A teacher should not issue more than one reprimand every four to five minutes. Second, if a consequence is indicated, then it should be delivered. However, consequences should be pre-planned and reasonable. They should not be invented on the spot while a teacher is angry at the child's misbehavior (if this happens, teachers tend to be overly punitive). Third, a teacher should keep track of the number of reprimands he/she delivers in comparison to the number of reinforcing statements. The rate of reinforcement should be four times as high as the rate of reprimands. Fourth, a set of presentation variables is important in the effective delivery of reprimands. These variables describe how a teacher actually gives a reprimand. Important factors are the distance from the student when a reprimand is given, how much time a student is given to respond to a reprimand, how the teacher faces the student, the type of voice that a teacher uses, and the emotionality of the teacher. Each of these variables is discussed here; a recap appears at the end of this module.

Format: Do not use a question or "Let's" format (e.g., "Isn't it time to do your work?" or "Let's get to work."). Instead, use a standard request or reprimand (e.g., "It is time to do your work now," or "Please do your work.").

Start Requests: The more positive your requests are, the more effective. It is better to tell students what you want them to do, not what you don't want them to do. For example, "Please start your arithmetic assignment," is better than, "Please stop talking."

Time: Wait approximately three to five seconds after you make the request or reprimand for a student to start complying. Do not say anything to the student during this time; simply wait. The temptation is to re-issue the command (unnecessarily) or to issue a new command. Approximately 40% of the time, teachers unnecessarily interrupt during this three to five second period.

Only Twice: State the reprimand or request only twice. If one reprimands or requests more than twice, the student becomes conditioned to repeated requests.

Distance: Teacher proximity to the student should be approximately three feet. (The average teacher issues a reprimand from 20 feet.) Long distance requests and reprimands have less impact.

Circulate: The more a teacher randomly circulates in a classroom, the more effective his/her requests will be. Ineffective teachers stay glued to their desks.

Eye Contact: Making eye contact with the student or asking him/her to look in your eyes will improve reprimand or request effectiveness. Poor teachers do not make eye contact and are often absorbed in other eye-catching tasks (e.g., reading, writing on the board) when they make a reprimand or request.

Touching: Softly touching a student's shoulder just before issuing a reprimand or request also helps to gain his/her attention. However, touching a secondary student or explosive student is not recommended.

> The more a teacher randomly circulates in a classroom, the more effective his/her requests will be.

Firm Voice: A request or command should be issued in a firm voice. This does not mean a yelling, cajoling, pleading, or humoring voice.

Soft Instead of Loud: It is better to issue a reprimand in a firm but soft voice at a three-foot distance than to give a loud reprimand. Loud reprimands are generally given at distances greater than three feet, and they tend to distract other students.

Nonemotional: It is always better to give a nonemotional reprimand than an emotionally loaded one. Calling a student a name (e.g., "My, you are so lazy, now get to work,"), making threats, or becoming angry are very ineffective.

Proximal Request and Reinforcers: It sometimes helps to give requests to other students sitting near the unmotivated student before issuing a request to the difficult student. For example, issue a request to a normally cooperative student, wait for the student to comply, reinforce him/her, and then issue a request to the more problematic student. Similarly, it helps to spontaneously reinforce the surrounding students who are already complying before issuing a request to the difficult student. A good rule to remember is that at least two positive social reinforcers should be given to complying students before each reprimand or request is given to a noncomplying student.

Momentum: It often helps to encourage an unmotivated student to respond by issuing positive and fun requests before issuing a more difficult one. In a sense, the teacher builds up a "momentum" of compliance before more difficult requests are made. For example, ask the unmotivated student to pass out the class worksheets before issuing a request to start working on the assignment. Or, students might be given directions for a pleasant activity or game before more challenging assignments are made. A common mistake made by teachers is to review or try to review the previous day's difficulties first thing in the morning, and then to instruct the students to work. This has the opposite effect of compliance momentum.

Description and Specificity: It is more effective to specifically describe the performance the teacher wants rather than to give global statements. For example, it is better to state, "Do the even math problems on page 38," instead of "Do your work that I told you to do." Specificity increases compliance.

Positive Consequences: If a student complies with a request or reprimand, it is important to socially reinforce the student. It is a mistake to let sleeping dogs lie. Some teachers state, "He is following my directions now, and I do not want to interrupt him or he might stop." This is wrong for two reasons. First, the student is less likely to complete the requested task if he/she is not socially reinforced. Second, in the future the student is less likely to comply with the teacher's requests.

Negative Consequences: Not all students comply with the teacher's requests, and sometimes a mild negative consequence is needed. For example, if a student does not comply, he/she might get a check on the board as a warning, lose his/her recess, or be given a brief time-out period. Frequently, teachers threaten students and do not carry out the consequences. Do not threaten. Have preplanned consequences ready for students and follow through with them every time students have earned them.

Precision Requests

A precision request is a sure-fire recipe for student compliance. It can be used to prompt appropriate behaviors or to stop inappropriate behaviors in the classroom. In addition to the steps described for effective reprimands, the following rules are specific to the use of precision requests:

1. If a second request is needed, use the key word, "need."
2. If the request is followed, use a social reinforcer (e.g., praise).
3. If the request is not followed, use a mild preplanned negative consequence.
4. After the negative consequence has been delivered, return to Rule #3 and repeat request cycle again or until the student follows the request.

An important aspect of using a precision request is that the teacher has preplanned, mild negative consequences. Effective negative consequences include the loss of a privilege such as free time, recess, or eating lunch in the lunchroom. Checks on the board are also a good system. For example, for the first occurrence of not working, the student's name and a check are placed on the board. For each additional

Specificity increases compliance.

check, the student loses five minutes of recess until the whole recess is gone. During recess, the student should make up the academic work.

Time-out can be used with precision requests for very disruptive behaviors such as arguing, property destruction, or tantrums (e.g., "I need you to stop arguing with me."). If time-out is used, it is important to restate the command "I need you to . . ." after the student leaves time-out. If the student refuses, the teacher should re-implement the time-out procedure.

However, time-out is a poor consequence for academic motivation problems. Frequently, students would rather be in time-out than do their academic work. A good compromise is to have the student bring a favored toy or object from home. For each check on the board, the toy stays in time-out (i.e., on the teacher's desk) and the student has to wait (while doing academics) during recess or free time for the toy to come out of time-out.

Troubleshooting Precision Requests

PROBLEM: *Precision requests may have been working initially, but have lost their effectiveness.*

> **Solution:** This generally means that they have been over-used, that the teacher is not reinforcing enough when students follow requests, or that the teacher does not consistently deliver effective preplanned consequences for noncompliance.

PROBLEM: *After the implementation of precision requests, the student's behavior becomes worse.*

> **Solution:** This usually means that the student is using coercion with the teacher. In other words, the student becomes worse, hoping that the teacher will withdraw the request. The teacher must stand firm and follow through with the precision requests and the preplanned consequences. If he/she does not, worse behavior on the student's part will be reinforced.

PROBLEM: *The student becomes physically aggressive when he/she is issued a precision request.*

Solution: This is the same as the problem immediate preceding. The student is using coercion on the teacher in the form of physical force. The teacher must have a preplanned consequence, which may necessitate that student being removed from the room. However, it is important to remember that when the student returns, the teacher must re-issue the "I need you to . . ." request. If he/she does not, the student will learn to escape or avoid a teacher's request by being removed from the classroom.

PROBLEM: *A student tries to be funny or make jokes each time the teacher issues a precision request.*

Solution: This is another form of coercion, in which the student is trying to escape or avoid the request. The teacher must not laugh or smile and must remain unemotional with a neutral look on his/her face. If the student does not comply within five seconds of the "I need you to . . . ," then the teacher should implement the preplanned consequences.

PROBLEM: *Many students will wait until the last second and then say "OK, I'll do it."*

Solution: By doing this, the student is trying to coerce the teacher into delaying the implementation of the preplanned consequence. The teacher should implement the consequence, and when the consequence is over, re-issue the "I need you to . . ." statement.

PROBLEM: *The student begins the requested behavior within three to five seconds after the precision request, but then stops doing the work or does it too slowly.*

Solution: The precision request may be stated as "I need you to do your math assignment in the next 30 minutes." It may help to set a kitchen timer. If the student is not finished within the specified time frame, the teacher should implement the consequence and re-issue the request with another time limit.

PROBLEM *The student will respond to the "I need you to . . ." request, but will not respond the first time to other simple requests made by the teacher during the day.*

Solution: The student may even get legalistic and say, "I don't have to do it because you didn't use the word need." The way to avoid this is to use the formal "I need you to . . . " request for a week for all initial requests. When the student is responding well, the teacher should inform him/her that sometimes he/she will use the word "need" and sometimes he/she will not. In either case, the preplanned consequences will be used for not complying. The teacher should not negotiate or overly explain this point.

PROBLEM: *The student starts to use the "I need you to . . . " request with the teacher and expects him/her to respond.*

Solution: The student may say it is only fair for him/her to use the precision request with the teacher or other students because the teacher uses it with him/her. The teacher can let the student know the world is not fair and if he/she uses the precision request with the teacher, then the teacher will automatically use the preplanned consequence with him/her (e.g., name on the board). The teacher should not argue this point or succumb to the fairness argument.

PROBLEM: *The student does not respond and says he/she does not understand the "I need you to . . ." request.*

Solution: The teacher should explain the request sequence and preplanned consequence once or twice—no more is needed. The teacher will, of course, make sure that the precision requests are specific and descriptive. If the student still has problems, then it is probably a ploy to get out of the request or consequence.

The teacher should stay with the program and implement the request sequence for about a week. If the student improves, the teacher should stick with the procedure. If there is no improvement in a week, the teacher should check: (1) The way he/she gives the precision request, (2) His/her reinforcement rate, and (3) The potency of the preplanned consequence. The teacher should explain the procedure again, increase the reinforcement rate for appropriate behavior (i.e., to at least one positive comment each 15 minutes), and change the preplanned consequence (i.e., change a check on the board for loss of recess time to a call home to a parent or a time-out procedure).

When precision requests are not working, check the following: (1) The teacher's positive reinforcement rate to the whole class, (2) The teacher's distance from the student when making the request, (3) Eye contact with the student, (4) The teacher's circulating in the classroom, (5) The loudness and emotionality of the teacher's voice, (6) Whether the student is given enough time (three to five seconds) to respond to the request, and (7) Whether there is consistent follow through with preplanned consequences.

Cautions

The biggest problem with the use of precision requests or effective reprimands is when a teacher becomes emotionally excited and does not have preplanned, negative consequences in place. If this happens, teachers tend to punish too harshly or implement very unrealistic consequences (e.g., "You are grounded for the rest of the month.") Staying calm and knowing exactly what the next action will be is critically important to the success of this procedure.

Case Study

Jeffery is an eight-year old in the third grade. He has had constant problems with staying on-task and finishing his work, particularly his math sheets. In addition, Jeffery bothers other children and brings their work rates down. Nothing seems to reward Jeffery for staying on-task and finishing his work. He would rather daydream and clown around with the children who sit near him.

His teacher decided to try a series of simple precision requests to improve Jeffery's academics and his problem behavior with other children. First, the teacher targeted the 30 minutes of in-seat math work on which to implement the precision requests. During this time, she increased her positive comments to Jeffery and the boys sitting near him for doing their work. In addition, the teacher made sure she circulated

around the classroom during the math period instead of trying to do work at her desk. Initially, this had a positive effect, but within a week Jeffery was up to his old behaviors.

The second step was to implement the precision request intervention. The teacher stated that off-task students would be requested to work with the "I need you to . . . " request. If anyone continued to not work, their name would be placed on the board with a check beside it. For each check, the student would miss five minutes of their recess and have to stay in and do additional academic math work. If there were no names on the board for the whole class, the whole class could have an additional five minutes of recess. The teacher explained the procedure twice. When Jeffery tried to argue, she simply stated that there could be no negotiations.

During the first day of the precision request intervention, things went well. There were no names on the board, and the whole class enjoyed an additional five minutes of recess. However, on the second day, Jeffery strayed off-task and started talking with a neighbor. Immediately, the teacher went up to Jeffery (i.e., within three feet of him), touched his shoulder, made eye contact, and stated, "Class, please do your math." This had a positive effect on Jeffery and all the boys near him. However, Jeffery soon was off-task again, and the teacher now said, "Class, now I need you to work." Again, he began to work; however, he soon went off-task. He also walked up to the pencil sharpener without permission. Immediately, the teacher put his name on the board with a check. Jeffery stated that this was unfair, since he was starting to work but needed his pencil sharpened. The teacher, without comment, put another check by his name and then walked over and looked him in the eye. Instead of arguing, Jeffery got to work. However, a boy nearby snickered. The teacher calmly walked up to the board, wrote down this boy's name with a check, and then walked over near him. After everyone had been working for five minutes, the teacher picked a student near Jeffery and praised him for working well. Then after a brief time, the teacher made the same comment about Jeffery.

References

Heller, M.S. & White, M.A. (1975). Rates of approval and disapproval to higher and lower ability classes. *Journal of Educational Psychology, 67,* 769-800.

Van Houten, R. & Doley, D.M. (1983). Are social reprimands effective? In S. Axelrod & J. Apsche (Eds.), *The effects of punishment on human behavior* (pp. 45-70). New York: Academic Press.

Van Houten, R., Nau, P., MacKenzie-Keating, D., Sameoto, D., & Calavecchia, B. (1982). An analysis of some variables influencing the effectiveness of reprimands. *Journal of Applied Behavior Analysis, 15,* 65-83.

White, M.A. (1975). Natural rates of teacher approval and disapproval in the classroom. *Journal of Applied Behavior Analysis, 8,* 367-372.

Ten Variables That Affect Compliance

1. **Format:** The use of questions instead of direct requests reduces compliance. For example, "Would you please stop teasing?" is less effective than "I need you to stop teasing."

2. **Distance:** It is better to make a request from up close (i.e., one meter, one desk distance) than from longer distances (i.e., seven meters, across the classroom).

3. **Eye Contact:** It is better to look into the child's eyes or ask the child to look into your eyes than to not make eye contact.

4. **Two Requests:** It is better to give the same request only twice than to give it several times (i.e., nag). Do not give many different requests rapidly (e.g., "Please give me your homework, behave today, and do not tease the girl in front of you.")

5. **Loudness of Request:** It is better to make a request in a soft but firm voice than in a loud voice (i.e., yelling when making a request to get attention).

6. **Time**—Give the student time to comply after giving a request (three to five seconds). During this short interval, do not converse with the child (arguing, excuse making), restate the request, or make a different request. Simply look the child in the eyes and wait for compliance.

7. **Start Requests:** It is more effective to make positive requests of a child to start an appropriate behavior (e.g., "Please start your arithmetic assignment."), than to request him/her to stop an inappropriate behavior (e.g., "Please stop talking.").

8. **Nonemotional Requests:** It is better to control negative emotions when making a request (e.g., yelling, name calling, guilt-inducing statements, and roughly handling a child.) Emotional responses decrease compliance and make the situation worse.

9. **Descriptive Requests:** Requests that are positive and descriptive are better than ambiguous or global requests (i.e., "Please sit in your chair, with your feet on the floor, hands on your desk, and look at me," is better than "Pay attention.")

10. **Reinforce Compliance:** It is too easy to request a behavior from a child and then ignore the positive result. If you want more compliance, genuinely reinforce it.

Teacher Praise

by Tony Loveless, M.S., Iron School District, Cedar City, Utah

Introduction

Throughout our society, one of the most common forms of positive reinforcement is praise. Teachers who make effective use of praise improve classroom atmosphere and reduce behavior disruptions so that all students benefit from a positive educational experience.

Praise is any verbal or non-verbal action by the teacher that indicates approval of or satisfaction with student behavior. Examples are phrases such as, "That's good working," "I appreciate your time on-task," "You must feel proud of yourself for your effort," and so forth.

O'Leary and O'Leary (1977) concluded that, "Teacher attention is perhaps the most basic of all influences on student behaviors and the systematic use of attention should characterize every teacher's classroom repertoire" (p. 55). Wyatt and Hawkins

(1987) and Vasta (1981) report that it has become commonplace to teach prospective teachers about the importance of contingent approval. Unfortunately, training them to actually use it appears to be less common. Because it can be so effective, it is important for teachers to learn how to use praise to their advantage in their classrooms.

A number of researchers have found the use of teacher praise and attention to be helpful in improving

OBJECTIVES

By the end of this module, you will know:

- Advantages of using teacher praise.
- What makes teacher praise effective.
- Steps to enhance the effectiveness of praise.
- Why/how to monitor student target behaviors when using praise as an intervention.

on-task time, study skills, and academic grades while also reducing behavioral disruptions. A study by Shutte and Hopkins (1970) showed an increase in the following of instructions, while Witmer, Bernstein, and Dunham (1971) and Madsen, Becker, and Thomas (1968) showed how teacher praise, when paired with a performance contingency, could be used to decrease inappropriate behavior. Thomas, Becker, and Armstrong (1968) report that the actual rates of teacher praise are very low despite the effectiveness of this procedure. This is supported by White (1975), who indicated a continual decrease in frequency of teacher praise with each successive grade level. White (1975) also reported that this appears to at least partially explain why students seem to experience the "disenchantment" or "loss of sense of joy in school" that she said knowledgeable observers report to occur after the first grade.

> If you always do what you've always done, you'll always get what you've always got.

annoying are socially unskilled and do not set themselves up to be socially reinforced. Usually, these students are starving for appropriate recognition from their teachers. It is unfortunate that many teachers working with socially unskilled students underutilize praise. One reason for this is that many students who are in need of reinforcement do not often demonstrate behavior for which teachers feel they can deliver genuine praise.

Remember, though, that "if you always do what you've always done, you'll always get what you've always got." Therefore, trying something different with these students is probably to their benefit as well as to the teacher's. In the long run, students who benefit most from this type of intervention usually occupy more teacher time to deal with their inappropriate behavior than it would take for the teacher to consciously and effectively praise their appropriate behavior.

What Makes Praise Effective?

A nice feature about teacher praise is that it does not take a lot of training, complex materials, forms, or data collection prowess. In fact, of all the interventions available for classroom use by a teacher, praise is probably the least cumbersome.

A basic requirement, however, is that the teacher be able to leave his/her desk or worktable and move around the classroom so that he/she is in a position to praise appropriate behavior and academic efforts as they naturally occur. White (1975) reported that "classrooms that demonstrated a high level of praise indicated a high level of time on-task." The converse was also true; teachers who used little praise, or used more disapproval, had a lower percentage of time on-task for the class as a whole.

A short refresher course on the basics of positive reinforcement may be in order for a teacher to effectively implement praise strategies. Understanding the principles underlying the use of positive reinforcement is conducive to rewarding appropriate behavior at appropriate times. The use of praise, a social reinforcer, is probably one of the most important reinforcers for any human being. A smile, a comment about a good job or a good effort, and an expression of appreciation for a person's willingness to try are all examples of social reinforcers. Many students with disabilities who are off-task or

Steps for Implementing Praise

The I-Feed-V rules apply when delivering praise. These rules are as follows:

I stands for "immediately." The more immediately the praise is delivered, the more effective it will be. The teacher must also remember that the younger the student, the more immediate the praise must be to be effective.

F stands for "frequently" reinforcing the student. This is extremely important when trying to shape or develop a new behavior. Appropriate behaviors are shaped much more quickly with frequent praise than with less frequent, intermittent praise. The most common mistake made by a teacher is giving too few praise statements. The standard rule is 24-six. This means that the teacher should deliver at least 24 reinforcers or praise statements across six hours of school time. This would work out to be approximately one reinforcer every 15 minutes.

E The first "E" stands for "enthusiasm." A positive verbalization associated with what a student is doing has to be perceived as sincere to be effective. Monotonic verbalizations of, "Good job," soon lose their effectiveness. A student must genuinely feel that the teacher approves and is pleased with the effort being made.

A number of teachers feel that appropriate behaviors should just be demonstrated by students on their own. For the most part, they will be. However, many at-risk students will perform better when they receive enthusiastic praise for developing and demonstrating appropriate behaviors.

E The second "E" stands for "eye contact." It is very important for the teacher to look the student in the eye when delivering praise. Proximity to the student is important so that good eye contact can be maintained; obviously, it is somewhat more difficult to maintain good eye contact from across the room. In either case, it is helpful to call the student by name to prompt him/her to look at the teacher before the praise statement is delivered.

D stands for "describe the behavior." It is necessary to specifically describe the behavior that is being praised. Otherwise, students may not know why they are being praised or may think they are being praised for something else. Describing the desired behavior also helps students to self-monitor their behavior in the future. An example of this is, "Billy, I sure like the way you stayed in your seat for the last five minutes." Another important point is that by describing the behaviors, the teacher lets other students in the class know what is desired.

V stands for "variety." This is an important concept, since students will quickly tire of the same old comments such as, "Good job," "I like that," "Very nice." Praise that is not varied and maintained with enthusiasm will become tiresome, boring, and will rapidly lose its effectiveness. One must be creative in administering praise.

> Praise that is not varied and maintained with enthusiasm will become tiresome, boring, and will rapidly lose its effectiveness.

Monitoring student progress during praise intervention is a must and is relatively simple. A tally sheet kept on a note tablet can give an indication to the teacher as to whether or not a student is decreasing out-of-seat behaviors or increasing completion of assignments. Comparing grades before and after the implementation is another way of monitoring the effectiveness of the intervention on academics. A student who has consistently failed assignments in the past and who begins to earn passing grades is obviously making progress.

Data on student behaviors during this program are necessary in order for the teacher to evaluate progress and make appropriate decisions regarding how to proceed. If adequate progress has been made, and target behaviors are maintained at appropriate levels, the teacher will want to begin to systematically fade the praise to a lower, more manageable level. Once the effectiveness of using praise has been shown with a particular student, it can be used in other areas throughout the day to increase appropriate academic and behavioral performances.

Another variation of using praise effectively is to pair it with disapproval or mild reprimands. The following rules apply when using reprimands in conjunction with praise:

1. Reprimands should only be used when the reinforcement rate from the teacher and classroom personnel exceeds the reprimand rate. This means that the number of praise statements should exceed the number of reprimands. A current guideline is about 4:1. For every one reprimand, there should be four praise statements. If the ratio is too low, the teacher must find more behaviors for which to praise students.

2. Reprimands should not be over-used. One reprimand every four or five minutes should be the maximum. Of course, even this rate would mean that an effective teacher should average four times as many praise statements during that time. It is important to remember that a teacher who uses reprimands more than praise soon loses control of the class.

Cautions

Teacher praise alone (or paired with mild reprimands) may not be effective for some students who do not care what the teacher likes or appreciates. In these cases, the teacher may need to initially pair the praise with some more tangible reinforcement or with a token economy, so that the praise will take on reinforcing qualities by association with something the student does find desirable. Students may become praise-dependent, meaning that they only produce work or appropriate behavior as long as the teacher is in the immediate vicinity or is recognizing their effort. To avoid this problem, the teacher should not stay at one student's desk too long or too often, but should circulate within the classroom.

Praise should never be faded out completely, but an attempt should be made to gradually reduce it to levels that are considered normal within a classroom setting. Older students may find verbal praise from the teacher undesirable, even when a teacher uses praise with a variety of students for a variety of reasons. For some students, public praise is more embarrassing than it is rewarding. For these students, it is suggested that praise be given on a one-to-one basis in an unobtrusive manner. The teacher may do this by standing beside the classroom door as the student enters or exits or even by a short note written on the student's paper.

Troubleshooting With Teacher Praise

PROBLEM: *Student progress on the target behaviors has not been adequate.*

> **Solution**: Praise alone may not be sufficiently reinforcing to the student. The teacher may need to initially pair it with the use of a token economy or tangible reinforcement to make it effective. In this case, once the target behavior has stabilized at appropriate levels, the additional reinforcer should be gradually faded, leaving only the praise.

PROBLEM: *Student behavior is actually getting worse.*

> **Solution**: The teacher should monitor the student (or ask an aide to take data) and find out whether more attention/verbal remarks are directed toward the student's inappropriate behaviors. The teacher may inadvertently have been increasing inappropriate behavior in this manner. If this is the case, the teacher can correct the problem by using praise so that the desired 4:1 praise to mild reprimand rates exist.

Case Study

Rose is an eight-year old, third grade student who has a history of incomplete assignments and poor study habits. Baseline observations during the math and spelling periods produced a mean rate of about 30% time on-task, fluctuating from 0% to 71%. Her off-task behaviors included laying her head on the desk, taking off her shoes, talking, and being out of her seat.

On the day the teacher was to first praise Rose's on-task behaviors, Rose did not study at all, and the teacher was thus unable to provide any praise for the behavior. Therefore, beginning with the second praise session, the teacher praised the behavior that approximated time on-task, such as, getting out pencils, paper, or opening the book to the correct page. Once these behaviors were praised, time on-task quickly followed. By the third praise session, time on-task had risen to 57%. During the fourth session, however, time on-task dropped to about 25%. An analysis of the data indicated that Rose had out-of-seat behavior in order to have her papers checked and to ask questions. Thereafter, the teacher ignored Rose when she approached but praised her immediately when she raised her hand while seated. There was an immediate drop in out-of-seat behavior and a concurrent increase in time on-task. During the last ten praise sessions, on-task behavior ranged between 74% and 92%, with the rate of 81% for the entire period. A high rate of time on-task was maintained after the 13th praise session.

During the fourth (reversal) session, on-task behavior was recorded only about 29% of the time. However, resumption of praise for time on-task immediately increased the behavior to 72% of the observed interval, with the level of time on-task remaining steady after the second praise session.

References

Madsen, C.H., Becker, W.C., & Thomas, D.R. (1968). Rules, praise, ignoring: Elements of elementary classroom control. *Journal of Applied Behavior Analysis, 1*(2), 139-150.

O'Leary, K.D. & O'Leary, S.G. (1977). *Behavior modification with children. Classroom management: The successful use of behavior modification* (2nd ed.). New York: Pergamon Press.

Shutte, R.C. & Hopkins, B. L. (1970). The effects of teacher attention on following instructions in a kindergarten class. *Journal of Applied Behavior Analysis, 3*, 117-122.

Thomas, D.A., Becker, W.C., & Armstrong, M. (1968). Production and elimination of disruptive classroom behavior by systematically varying teacher's behavior. *Journal of Applied Behavior Analysis, 1*, 35-45.

Vasta, R. (1981). On token rewards and real dangers: A look at the data. *Behavior Modification, 5*, 129-140.

White, M.S. (1975). Natural rates of teacher approval and disapproval in the classroom. *Journal of Applied Behavior Analysis, 8*, 367-372.

Witmer, J., Bernstein, A., & Dunham, R. (1971). The effects of verbal approval and disapproval upon the performance of third and fourth grade children on four subtests of the WISC. *Journal of School Psychology, 9*, 347-357.

Wyatt, J. & Hawkins, R. (1987). Rates of teachers' verbal approval and disapproval. *Behavior Modification, 11*(1), 27-51.

Contracting to Enhance Motivation

by William R. Jenson, Ph.D., University of Utah, and H. Kenton Reavis, Ed.D., Utah State Office of Education

Introduction

When the word "contract" is used, we generally think of corporate mergers, or of sports stars signing agreements for millions of dollars. However, contracts have an everyday meaning for most of us. When we buy cars, we sign contract agreements for repayment. Even a car's warranty is a contract for service if there is a problem with the car. When we get married, the marriage vows are a form of contract and the marriage license is legal proof of the exchange of those vows. Even when we took our teaching position, most of us signed an employment contract which specified our salary and benefits for an exchange of services. Most of these teaching contracts also had a penalty clause for quitting the job without proper notice.

We use contracts for many adult behaviors because they are explicit and they set expectations. For simi-

lar reasons, they can be used in classrooms. Contracts can be particularly helpful for enhancing academic motivation in students for whom expectations are important and explicit exchanges of consequences are needed.

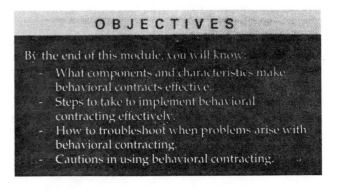

OBJECTIVES

By the end of this module, you will know:
- What components and characteristics make behavioral contracts effective.
- Steps to take to implement behavioral contracting effectively.
- How to troubleshoot when problems arise with behavioral contracting.
- Cautions in using behavioral contracting.

Are Behavioral Contracts Effective?

The answer to this question is yes, within limits. Clearly, the research literature has demonstrated that contracts can be effective in improving academic productivity in a classroom, homework completion, classroom behavior, and school attendance. In order for a contract to be effective, the student must be capable of producing the required behavior (at least), and the delay in delivering a positive reward must not be too long. Examples of using contracts to improve academic motivation and classroom behavior are provided here.

Academics

Contracting has been used in several circumstances to improve academic motivation and performance in students. Kirschenbaum, Dielman, and Karloy (1982) contracted with high school dropouts to increase classroom participation and homework production in earning their GEDs. The simple reward used in this study was a positive letter signed by the teachers and directors of the school, written to the students' counselors (the counselors controlled the students' finances). In this study, appropriate classroom participation and academic gains, as measured by the IOWA Test of Basic Skills (ITBS), increased. However, homework improvements were only slight.

In a similar study, Kelley and Stokes (1982) contracted with 13 youths enrolled in a vocational training program for disadvantaged youths. Students were paid according to how they fulfilled their academic productivity goals. The students had been paid to attend the program; however, the teacher indicated that minimal progress was made. The administrator of the program reported that repeated threats, including coercive threats to be dropped from the program, had no impact on the students' academic motivation. However, making the students' payments dependent on academic production dramatically increased the number of academic items completed by the students.

Behavior

Contracting has also been used to improve several types of behavior including substance abuse, school attendance, and appropriate classroom behavior. A unique approach is the contract-based "Student Oriented Classroom" (Besalel-Azrin, Azrin, & Armstrong, 1977). The procedures were used in a fifth grade classroom in which the teacher requested assistance for dealing with fighting and uncooperative behavior from the students. The procedures included establishing basic classroom rules for the students and teacher. The contracting component involved giving students daily feedback (one to three minutes) on their progress. Student classroom privileges were based on their individual contract performance in following the classroom rules, and on a weekly conference (five minutes) on their progress. This program also included a system of polite interaction rules between students and teacher, a chance for students to make up a mistake before losing a privilege (overcorrection), parent feedback on contract progress, and a public progress display of the contract goals. Progress as measured by students' perceptions was a 67% reduction in problems and by teacher perceptions a 90% reduction.

What Makes Behavioral Contracts Effective?

There are a number of characteristics of behavioral contracts which must be present in order for them to be effective. These are:

Agreeing: This means that both parties, the teacher (or parent) and the child, have negotiated what consequence will be given for what type of behavior. Negotiation suggests an exchange of proposals and counter-proposals between parties. The negotiation aspect of a contract is one of its major advantages, particularly in working with adolescents who want to be adult-like and independent. Negotiations should not be one-sided in the sense that one person dictates terms to the other person.

Formal Exchange: This part of the definition indicates that a behavior will be produced, and then a reinforcer or reward will be given. The contracting equation is Behavior = Reward. Relaxing the behavior requirements in the middle of a contract is generally a mistake, and not giving the agreed-upon reward after the behavior has been produced is always a mistake. Also, it is always a mistake to give the reward before the behavior is produced.

Reward or Reinforcement: The positive consequence is frequently the motivating component of a contract. Without some type of reward or reinforcement, most children will not complete the requirements of a contract. However, other consequences can also be implemented with contracts. For example, penalty clauses can be implemented if a behavior is not produced within a certain time frame. In addition, bonus rewards can enhance motivation if a behavior is exceptionally well done or is produced before a deadline.

Behavior: The negotiating and defining of the behavioral expectations of a contract can be one of its most important functions. The behavior should be defined so that it is objective (i.e., can be measured easily or seen). The behavioral definition should also include the standard that is expected (e.g., a "B" grade or better) and the time deadlines (e.g., by the end of next Friday). A behavior that is objectively defined up to a standard with time deadlines is an essential component of a contract.

In addition to these characteristics, there are several approaches that can enhance the effectiveness of contracting with unmotivated students. These approaches generally involve combining contracting with other techniques.

Goal Setting: Contracting can be combined with having students set their own academic goals. If this procedure is used, a bonus for reaching the goal sooner and a penalty clause for not reaching the goal on time can be added.

Public Posting: This procedure has already been mentioned in combination with written contracts. The procedure should include contracting for improvements and displaying the contracts on a public bulletin board. Written contracts that are publicly posted can be enhanced by spotlighting a "Contract of the Week"; having students design and do the artwork on their individual contracts; or having a displayed column of squares, with each square that a student colors signifying one step closer to his/her contract goal.

Group Contingencies: A contract can be designed for a total classroom or for teams instead of an individual student. Caution should be taken in implementing a group contract to make sure that each child is capable of contributing to the contract goal. An example of a puclicly posted group contingency might be for the teachers to designate class teams which race toward a city on a United States map. For example, it might be that the first team to go from Los Angeles to New York wins. Each completed student assignment contributes to so many miles (i.e., a grade of 100% = 100 miles; 75% = 75 miles). Speeding tickets can be given for tardies or not turning in homework. Bonuses can be given on random days for the most mileage earned.

Homenotes: Contracts can be included in a homenote program. For example, when a student accumulates four weeks' worth of perfect homenotes (all four weeks do not have to be in a row), he/she receives an agreed-upon reward or earns a mystery motivator.

Steps for Implementing Behavioral Contracting

STEP ONE

Defining the contract behavior(s) is the first step in implementing a contract. The behavior must be observable and measurable—in other words, things that a teacher can actually measure or see. Poor choices for contract behaviors include "improving classroom responsibility" or "showing more respect for others." Better alternatives are "hand in work by the end of the period without being asked" or "follow the classroom rules regarding classmates—talk in a calm voice, do not argue, do not fight, share toys." These are behaviors that can actually be seen and measured.

> Nothing kills the effectiveness of a contract faster for an unmotivated student than experiencing another academic failure.

It may be necessary to break a behavior into smaller steps for a contract, particularly if a student is academically unmotivated. For example, instead of contracting for 30 arithmetic problems, a teacher may ask for ten the first week, then 20 the second week, and finally 30 the third week. It is important to define and break up a behavior so the student is initially successful in earning the contract reward. Nothing kills the effectiveness of a contract faster for an unmotivated student than experiencing another academic failure.

STEP TWO

Selecting contract reinforcers is the next step in implementing a contract. It is important to remember that a teacher may list several items that a child might like. However, the child should participate in selecting reinforcers in the negotiation phase of setting up a contract. The basic rule in selecting contract reinforcers is that reinforcers should not take a lot of time to deliver, nor should they be expensive. It is better to use existing classroom rewards such as extra free time, being allowed to line up first for a week, being able to wear a hat in the classroom, a reserved parking space for older students, sitting next to a friend, or being the teacher's classroom aide. Treats, small toys, or classroom supplies (pencils, erasers, notebooks, etc.) may also be provided. One high school teacher persuaded community businesses to donate reinforcers such as gift certificates for five gallons of gasoline, free pizzas, and movie tickets. However, many of these items are large and comparatively expensive and should be used sparingly, or as bonuses for contracts.

STEP THREE

Defining the contract criterion is important and is often poorly done in contracts. The contract criterion is actually the definition of what is required before an exchange of reinforcement for behavior is given. Generally, contract criteria specify the amount of behavior, amount of reinforcer, and time limits. There are two basic contract criteria. These are consecutive criteria and cumulative criteria.

The poorer type of contract criterion is a consecutive criterion in which the behavior is required in an uninterrupted sequence. For example, the student may be told he/she will receive the contract reward if he/she earns a "B" or better on his/her arithmetic assignments for ten straight days. In this case, the student may have nine days of straight "B"s and receive a "C" on the tenth, thus not receiving the reward. Consecutive requirements are harsh and punishing for many unmotivated students.

A better type of contract criterion is a cumulative criterion in which the amount of behavior adds up with each success but does not count for failures. For example, the student may receive the contract reward when he/she earns ten "B"s or better on his/her arithmetic assignment. In this example, the student could have some days in which performance drops below a "B"; however, after he/she receives ten "B"s (with several lower grades in between) he/she receives the reward (e.g., Mon-"B"; Tue-"A"; Wed-"C"; Thur-"B"; Fri-"B"; Mon-"C"; Tue-"B"; Wed-"A"; Thur-"B"; Fri-"B"; Mon-"A"; Tue-"B" = Earn Contract Reward). Cumulative criteria are better because they allow the student some days in which he/she does not meet the criterion.

Time limits are explicit in most contracts. Many contracts are defined so that they pay off at the end of the week. However, contracts that go longer than two weeks are generally less effective because students cannot wait that long. A good approach is to pay off by at least the end of the week for students who have a cumulative criterion. For example, on Fridays (Pay Day), students with five or more completed "B" homework assignments can watch a movie video. Students who do not have the five must work on their assignments during the movie, but they can save the assignment from this week to count towards next week's contract.

STEP FOUR

For unmotivated students, it is often essential to include a bonus clause and a penalty clause. A bonus clause can be an extra incentive if a student does a particularly good job or beats a timeline. This can be important when a student takes an exceptionally long time to reach the contract's cumulative criterion. For example, a student will receive the contract reward when he/she is on time to class ten times (cumulative). A bonus will be given if the student is on time ten times in ten straight days with no tardies (consecutive). Often, a bonus payoff can be based on a combination of cumulative and consecutive criteria. The basic function of a bonus is to get a student to complete a criterion in the least amount of time.

Penalty clauses are also needed with some unmotivated students. It is best to initially design an all-positive contract. However, if the contract rewards are valued and the payoff time is short, and the contract still does not work, then a penalty clause is probably needed. It is best to design the penalty with broad time limits. For example, the student needs 15 homework assignments of "B" or better to receive the contract reward for November (based on daily homework assignments for a 20 day period). However, if the number is less than ten for the month of November, the student loses television privileges for a week. A penalty clause is needed to give added incentive when all else fails.

STEP FIVE

The negotiation phase of contracting can be critical in securing the active participation of an unmotivated student. Negotiation allows the student to have some ownership of the contract and its terms. In addition, negotiation increases the basic communication between teacher and student and can give the teacher insights into a student's motivation problems that may have been unknown in the past. For instance, a student may disclose a basic skill deficiency that he/she was embarrassed to previously admit.

> Students are generally interested in the terms, rewards, and progress made on their contracts.

The basic substeps of negotiation are:

1. Have a specific set of contract behaviors, rewards, and criteria to discuss with the student.

2 Indicate to the student why a contract is necessary and how you want it to help with the student's difficulty.

3. Indicate that several components of the contract are negotiable such as rewards, behaviors, and criteria. However, a contract is needed and its implementation is not negotiable.

4. Tell the student what you want for the contract behaviors, suggest reinforcers, and indicate criteria. Ask the student for input.

5. Be careful at this stage of negotiation. Often, students set unrealistically high standards for themselves. Tell the student you want to start slow and then expand.

6. Indicate to the student that you genuinely want the contract to work. However, if things do not improve, a penalty clause may be needed. The penalty clause can be negotiated with the student within certain limits.

7. Tell the student that the contract is open to renegotiation at any time. Give the sense that you value the student's input and will renegotiate difficult behaviors, reinforcers, and criteria.

Never threaten the negative terms of a contract. Remember, a unilateral contract is not a contract by definition because all parties have not agreed to the terms.

STEP SIX

Put the terms of the contract in writing. Some individuals feel that actually writing the contract is superfluous; however, a written document serves several important functions. First, by writing a contract which includes a description of all the necessary elements, the parties can avoid later misunderstandings. Writing and signing a contract clears up ambiguity and indicates agreement with the terms at the time that all parties signed the contract. Second, a good written contract should have a section which includes data on the student's progress. If the contract has a data section, it functions as a self-recording instrument which further enhances the contract's effectiveness. Third, written contracts should be displayed. Hanging contracts on walls, taping them on desks, putting them on bulletin boards, or having a special section of the classroom to display contracts improves the effectiveness of the contract through public posting. Students are generally interested in the terms, rewards, and progress made on their contracts.

A sample written contract form is provided at the end of this module, along with a list of the basic components of a good contract.

Troubleshooting Contracts

No technique will work in all situations with an unmotivated student. Although contracts have numerous advantages and work especially well with older students, there can be problems with their use.

PROBLEM: *The student starts out working hard and then loses motivation.*

> **Solution:** The reward payoff may be too distant in the future. This is one of the most frequent problems with contracts. Try to cut the time requirement in half.

PROBLEM: *The student appears confused and never really gets started.*

> **Solution:** This may be a problem of not defining the required behaviors carefully enough or of initially requiring too much of the target behavior. Be specific in defining the behavior. Discuss it thoroughly with the student. Make sure he/she understands the requirement. If necessary, model and role play the behaviors. If the child understands, but still has difficulty with the contract, then the requirement may be too demanding. Try reducing the behavior requirement for one week (i.e., half the problems, a "C" instead of a "B," five pages instead of ten). After at least one week during which the child has received a contract reward, you can gradually begin to increase the contract requirement.

PROBLEM: *After negotiations, checking the time period for delivery of the reward, checking the specificity of the behaviors, and at least one week of fulfilling the contract, the student still seems unmotivated and disinterested. This is particularly a problem if the student is passively unmotivated.*

> **Solution:** A penalty clause may be necessary to get the student to actively participate. This may involve soliciting the cooperation of a parent so that the student is penalized at home (e.g., going to bed early or losing television privileges). If the parent cannot cooperate, a student may have to receive a penalty at school, such as losing recess or free time.

PROBLEM: *The student excitedly starts out with the contract but becomes frustrated and anxious before finishing.*

> **Solution:** First, check the criterion. Frustration can result from too difficult an expectation. Also, check the type of criterion. Consecutive requirements cause frustration and should be changed to a cumulative criterion.

PROBLEM: *The student is openly defiant and will not participate: in the contract.*

> **Solution:** Indicate to the student that you want to negotiate the terms of the contract and you value his input. It may help a great deal to have a person who is important to the student participate in the negotiations, particularly if a penalty clause is set. People you may want to invite are parents, a coach, another favored teacher, counselor or parole officer. Make sure that the invited person supports the idea of a contract and will be helping with the negotiation of its terms.

PROBLEM: *The parent(s) offer extremely large rewards with too long a time period before they are delivered. It is not uncommon for parents to promise bicycles, four wheelers, trips, remote control vehicles and money to a student for greatly improving academic progress (e.g., bring your "D"s up to "A"s and "B"s in one semester).*

> **Solution:** Parents can be a real asset in helping to design a contract. Talk to the parent(s) and express your concern over the promised large reinforcer. Work out a list of smaller rewards with a much shorter delay

period and suggest using the large reward as an additional bonus.

Cautions

Caution is needed regarding the use of contracts, in that teachers and parents must realize that most contracts are behavior management systems with a delayed reward payoff system. The word delayed is stressed because most contracts provide rewards on a weekly or biweekly schedule.

When working with unmotivated students, excessive delay frequently destroys initial steps that are needed to get a student started. Contracts can be most useful when: (1) They are used as a way of fading out more frequent rewards, or after a student has started to work appropriately, or (2) They are used with older or more motivated students. Contracts with long delays can be a mistake for younger children or highly unmotivated students. In these cases, it is better to start with an hourly, twice daily, or daily reward system.

Teachers must also be aware that parents and other professionals working with a student may have objections to the use of contracting. The teacher must be prepared to effectively counter these objections before proceeding with contracting as an intervention. There are several objections that are commonly voiced. The first is that contracts are not needed if students would just be responsible. It is easy to answer this objection. First, unmotivated or behaviorally acting-out students are not responsible; thus, other techniques are needed to make certain they succeed. The other answer to this objection is that even responsible individuals may need contracts for important behaviors. We have already discussed the use of contracts in buying a car, marrying, and accepting a teaching position.

The second objection is that contracts act as an artificial crutch. Contracts should be designed to enhance initial motivation and should then be slowly faded out of use. However, it is better to use a tool such as a contract and make sure that a student makes academic progress rather than letting him/her fail.

The third objection is that contracts are complex and take too much time. A well-designed contract is like a good investment. Most sound financial investments take initial start-up capital in order to return greater dividends later. Similarly, a well-designed contract will initially take a little more time than simply doing nothing with the student. However, the dividends are much greater in improving the student's academic motivation, improved communication through negotiating the contract, and focusing teacher attention on student performance. In fact, contracts are one of the most efficient strategies a teacher can use with a student to improve academic motivation.

Case Study

Bubba is a sixth grade student with severe motivational and behavior problems. He has had particular problems in completing class assignments and has never turned in homework. He is defiant in class and often appears frustrated by academic tasks. Bubba's parents are interested, but his father works night shifts and his mother reports that she can do little with Bubba at home. She reports that, "Bubba just sits and watches television."

When the teacher interviewed Bubba in her office, he reported that he would like to do better in class but has difficulty getting started. Bubba also reported that he feels stupid around other students, particularly when doing his arithmetic problems. Simple probes show that Bubba has several skill deficit areas in arithmetic, especially in multiplication facts. When asked what he likes, Bubba reported liking television, candy, money, and recess time.

The teacher decided to design a contract with Bubba in which he can be paid off each day with a simple in-class reinforcer if he has done his multiplication sheet for the day. There are several reinforcers written on slips of paper that are put in a grab bag, and Bubba gets to randomly select one each day. A bonus is also given when Bubba scores 80% or better on three multiplication fact tests (cumulative criterion); these tests

are given at the end of each week. The bonus is a secret reinforcer placed in a mystery motivator envelope (a sealed envelope that contains the reinforcer written on a slip of paper). The mystery motivator is kept in the teacher's desk drawer and may include such items as a movie video the teacher rented, lunch at a fast food restaurant with Bubba's father, or a sleepover with a friend. If Bubba fails to complete his daily multiplication fact sheet, the teacher calls home and the television is locked up (using a small tool chest lock on the plug) for one day.

The contract was written and signed by Bubba and his parents. Bubba took an active role in negotiating the reinforcers and the amount of work to be done. He was not particularly happy about the penalty clause of losing television for not working, but he said he would go along with the "deal." The teacher posted the contract on the bulletin board along with other children's contracts.

In the first four weeks of the contract, Bubba has completed 80% of all assigned arithmetic sheets and has learned his times tables through the eights. He has received one bonus of a sleepover, and his parents have had to lock up the television set only three times.

References

Kirschenbaum, D.S., Dielman, J.S., & Karloy, P. (1982). Efficacy of behavioral contracting: Target behaviors, performance criteria, and settings. _Behavior Modification, 6_(4), 499-518.

Kelley, M.L. & Stokes, T.F. (1982). Contingency contracting with disadvantaged youths: Improving classroom performance. _Journal of Applied Behavioral Analysis, 15_(3),447-454.

Besalel-Azrin, V., Azrin, N.H., & Armstrong, D.M. (1977). The student-oriented classroom: A method of improving student conduct and satisfaction. _Behavior Therapy, 8_(2),193-204.

"I've got an offer you can't refuse . . ."

_____'s Contract
(name)

I agree to: _____

_____

_____

If I meet these conditions by _____, I earn the following
(date)

privilege(s): _____

_____

Contract default penalties: _____

_____

Perfect score/exceptional work bonus: _____

Signed: _____   Witness: _____

Parent: _____   Today's Date: _____

Basic Components of a Behavioral Contract

1.   Date the agreement begins, ends, or is renegotiated (at least one week; no more than three weeks for behaviorally disordered students).

2.   Behavior(s) targeted for change (measurable).

3.   Amount and kind of reward or reinforcer to be used.

4.   Schedule of reinforcer's delivery.

5.   Signatures of all those involved: student, parent(s), mediator, and teacher.

6.   Schedule for review of progress (daily is best).

7.   Bonus clause for sustained or exceptional performance.

8.   Statement of the penalties that will be imposed if the specified behavior is not performed.

Using Group Contingencies to Improve Academic Achievement

by William R. Jenson, Ph.D., University of Utah, and H. Kenton Reavis, Ed.D., Utah State Office of Education

Introduction

A group contingency is a system for the delivery of a contingency to an entire group, based upon the behavior of the individuals in that group. There are three basic types of group contingencies:

1. **Individual-All Group Contingency**: With this type of group contingency, the consequence for the entire group is based on the performance of one individual. There are two variations to this type of group contingency.

Variation 1
The student is selected and announced to the group at the beginning of the day. The

> **OBJECTIVES**
>
> By the end of this module, you will know:
> - The three basic types of group contingencies.
> - How to implement a group contingency procedure.
> - Ways to enhance a group contingency procedure.
> - How to solve problems that may arise when using group contingencies.

advantage of this variation is that the identified student is motivated to do well because his/her name has been made public. The disadvantage is that, if the student fails, he/she may receive negative peer feedback. Although negative feedback is rare, a teacher should take these precautions: (1) Make sure the student is capable of meeting the criterion; (2) If negative peer feedback occurs, the teacher should be prepared to respond to that behavior with a preplanned consequence (e.g., loss of recess or of a prized privilege for the student who gave the negative feedback); and, (3) Talk with the students before the group contingency is implemented and indicate that negative feedback will not be tolerated and that there will be consequences for the student or the group if negative feedback occurs. However, indicate that genuine encouragement and support for the student is much preferable.

Variation 2

With this variation, a student is randomly selected to determine if he/she meets the group contingency criterion. Once a student is selected, then it is determined if he/she met the criterion and, hence, if the group is to be rewarded. The major advantage with this variation is that each student in the group has an equal probability of being selected, so all students are motivated. It helps to put the selected name in a sealed envelope at the front of the class. At the end of the day, the envelope is opened and the name read. The disadvantage of this approach is that the unmotivated student most in need of the benefits of the group contingency has a small chance of being selected (unless the teacher periodically rigs the selection).

2. **Independent Group-Contingency**: In this second type of group contingency, each member of the group must individually earn a reward based on individual performance. The same performance is required for each group member, and the consequences are the same for each. For example, extra recess time is given to each student who correctly finishes 80% of his/her arithmetic assignment. If students fall below 80%, they do not receive the extra recess. The advantage of this approach is that one rule applies with one consequence for all students. It is easy to implement. However, the disadvantage is that this is not a true group interdependency. Each student independently works to meet his/her criterion so they can gain access to the group reward. Students are not dependent on each other's performance for the consequence. Thus, cooperation is reduced and the overall effectiveness is less than a true interdependent group contingency.

3. **Group-All Group Contingency**: This is a true interdependent group contingency in which the group consequence is dependent on the performance of the group as a whole. For example, all students in a classroom must behave, with no checks on the board, before the group gets an extra snack time. There are two basic variations of this group contingency:

Variation 1

In this variation, each member of the group must meet a criterion before the class is rewarded. The advantage to this approach is that it fosters cooperation and encouragement among students. However, there are two basic disadvantages. First, this is an ambitious standard for many students. It may be very difficult for all students to meet the criterion. A teacher should start with a lower standard and slowly move the standard up as students improve. For example, a teacher may allow three names on the board for inappropriate behavior the first week (if it reaches four names, the group would not be rewarded); then the second week move to two names; and, the third week, one name. The second disadvantage is that it may be difficult for a teacher to keep track of a total group standard. For instance, if the standard is that all students must complete 80% of their arithmetic assignment, then the teacher must grade all of the students' papers before it can be determined if the group earns the reward. If the teacher has difficulty tracking the entire group, then Variation #2 may be more appropriate.

Variation 2

With this variation, students are randomly selected and their performance is averaged. If the average exceeds the criterion, the whole group is rewarded. If the average is below the criterion, then the group loses the reward. For example, if 80% completion of all arithmetic problems is the criterion, then the teacher would randomly select three students from the class. He/she would grade their papers immediately and decide if the 80% criterion had been met. The major advantage of this approach is the ease of calculating the criterion. Also, this approach encourages students to exceed the criterion because one or two superior performances may help average out a failing performance. Again, the major disadvantage is the severity of the criterion. Some students may be capable and others incapable of meeting the standard. Teachers should start with a lower standard and slowly increase it as students begin to improve.

Are Group Contingencies Effective?

Group contingencies and their effects on school performance have been carefully examined for more than 20 years. Several studies show that group contingencies are effective in reducing many difficult school behaviors, including: classroom misbehavior (Barrish, Saunders, & Wolf, 1969), bus riding behavior (Greene, Bailey, & Barber, 1981), swearing (Salend & Meddaugh, 1985), aggression (Brown, Reschly, & Saber, 1974), disruptive library behavior (Fishbein & Wasik, 1981), and many others. They have also been used to improve academic behavior such as spelling (Baer & Richards, 1980) and arithmetic (Speltz, Shimamura, & McReynolds, 1982).

Classroom Behavior

A good example of using a group contingency to improve classroom behavior was presented by Cowen, Jones, and Bellack (1979) using a group contingency with a rule stated in the form "If you do . . . , then you receive . . . . " This study was conducted with five regular elementary classrooms (approximately 25 students in each) ranging from first grade through third grade. All of the classrooms were in the Rochester City School District and were selected on the basis of reported high rates of disruptive behavior. A simple contingency was set, in which a

> Group contingencies and their effects on school performance have been carefully examined for more than 20 years.

low probability behavior (i.e., academics) must first be exhibited before a high probability behavior (i.e., play time) could be obtained. In this study, students were allowed to vote on preferred classroom activities from a reinforcement menu just before the academic period (a reading circle or in-seat work). The reinforcers selected usually included such items as alphabet bingo, eraser tag, playing musical chairs, and so on. However, before the students could participate in these activities, they needed to accumulate 15 minutes of good work.

Three high rate disruptive behaviors were selected to be decreased with the group contingency. These behaviors were: (1) Out-of-seat, (2) Talking with neighbors, and (3) Off-task. Students in each classroom were told that when they had earned 15 minutes of accumulated good work during the 30-minute academic time, then they could have the remaining 15 minutes for the preferred activity. The teacher held a stopwatch that kept running as long as students were working appropriately. However, if a student engaged in any of the misbehaviors listed, the teacher stopped the watch.

In theory, if all the students were perfect, they could earn 15 minutes of preferred activity time out of the 30-minute academic period. However, for each student that engaged in an inappropriate behavior, that time was subtracted for the whole group until that student returned to work (i.e., the watch was not started until the student worked). The teacher used a three-step sequence when a student misbehaved or went off-task:

STEP ONE

Stated the misbehaving student's name so the whole class could hear it.

STEP TWO

Told the student what to do (e.g., "Stop talking and get back to work.").

STEP THREE

Held the stopwatch up, and indicated the watch was not running with such statements as, "The watch is stopped," or "You're killing time."

This procedure was very effective with all of the targeted misbehaviors.

Academic Behavior

A study by Speltz, Shimamura, and McReynolds (1982) describes individual contingency versus three different types of group contingencies that can be applied to improve academic motivation in students. In this study, 12 learning disabled students ranging in age from seven to ten were included. All students had difficulty with arithmetic, but the assigned problems were within their capability level. The goal was to increase practice time spent working problems, in order to improve proficiency. For the students, each problem resulted in one point. The points could then be exchanged for valued rewards.

Group Contingency—All Members: With this group contingency, the average number of points from each student was used to determine the number of points for the whole group. For example, the number of points earned by each student was then averaged with the group as a whole. This number of points was then given to each member of the group.

Group Contingency—Identified Responder: A member of the group was selected, and the number of points earned by that student was then given to each member of the group.

Group Contingency—Unidentified Responder: All the names of the students in the group were put into a cup. At the end of the academic period, a name was selected (but not revealed) and the number of points earned by the selected student was then given to each member of the group.

Each of the procedures was effective, with an average performance increase of 66%. Only one student in the group of 12 did not show discernable improvements. It is important to note that the side effects of using the group contingencies were very positive. Negative comments and behaviors were very low. In the Identified Responder group contingency where peer social pressure might be expected to be high, "not a single instance of negative behavior was directed at these children" (p. 543). In fact, spontaneous peer helping behavior was reported, in which peers helped each other structure the task. This is similar to other studies, in which the majority of students and teachers express satisfaction and a preference for a well-designed group contingency once it has been implemented.

Steps for Implementing a Group Contingency

A group contingency may be needed if the teacher thinks there is inappropriate peer influence, a need exists for teaching responsibility and cooperation, or the class size is large with limited resources. If so, there are several steps to implementing an effective group contingency. These steps are outlined here:

STEP ONE

A decision about the type of group contingency to be used is the first step in implementing the procedure. For most educational situations, a group-all group contingency probably is most useful to improve academic motivation for an entire classroom. The random checking variation is practical. For targeting a chronically unmotivated student, an individual-all group contingency is best. If this contingency is used, the teacher should be sensitive to negative student feedback and make sure the student is capable of doing the assigned academic work.

STEP TWO

After the type of group contingency has been selected, it becomes important to specify the target behavior. If an academic behavior is selected, it should be one that is easily graded and quantified (e.g., 80% or better). It is also better to start with a lower standard and slowly increase the criterion as the student becomes more skilled. Again, it is important to make sure that the student is capable of completing the task at the desired level.

The targeted problem should be a motivation problem. If a student is just learning a new academic skill and has not yet mastered it, a group contingency can make things worse. In this situation, the student should be reinforced for effort.

If classroom behaviors are selected for the target behaviors, they should be clearly observable and measurable. Poorly defined behaviors such

> If a student is just learning a new academic skill and has not yet mastered it, a group contingency can make things worse. In this situation, the student should be reinforced for effort.

as poor attitude, disrespect, or sullen behavior are to be avoided. More preferred behaviors that can be used with a group contingency are talk-outs, out-of-seat, or not following a teacher's directions.

STEP THREE

Once a target behavior has been selected, it is important to collect baseline data on the behavior before a group contingency is started. A baseline allows a teacher to set a reasonable criterion. For example, the teacher might record how many times per week a student turns in his/her homework. If the student turns it in only once, then the teacher might set the criterion at turning homework in three times during the first week and then slowly increase the criterion. Similarly, if a student routinely completes only 40% of the problems on a math sheet each day, the teacher might set the criterion at 60% for the first week and then increase the criterion. For inappropriate behaviors, if a classroom has 20 talk-outs as a group in a day, the teacher might set the criterion at ten per day the first week.

One mistake often made by teachers is to set the criterion too high. If this is done, it is frustrating, and it takes the group too long to receive a reward. It should be possible for the group to earn the reward daily, particularly when a group contingency is first started.

Variety and unpredictability can be important variables in using a reward system.

STEP FOUR

Before a group contingency is started, it is important for the teacher to discuss the procedure with the class and the school principal, and to inform parents and ask for permission to proceed. A parent letter with a permission form explaining the group contingency and asking for consent is important. The letter can detail the target behavior of the group contingency. Also, the letters can be written to emphasize the cooperative-responsibility aspect of the group contingency and the positive aspects of the program (i.e., the extra privileges the group will earn that they would ordinarily not receive).

STEP FIVE

Select the consequences to be used with the group contingency. Consequences should be primarily positive. That is, the students should receive something extra if they meet the criterion. A poorly-designed group contingency emphasizes negative consequences. A good approach in the selection of positive consequences is to have students vote on a selection from a menu. Variety and unpredictability can be important variables in using a reward system. For example, a mystery motivator incorporates both variety and unpredictability. This is simply a reward that is written on a piece of paper and put in a sealed envelope in front of the classroom. The students do not know exactly what they will get until they have reached the criterion. Other rewards can be chosen from a grab bag (a bag with several group rewards, from which one student selects without looking).

If negative consequences are used with a group contingency, it is better to have students work an extra period of time. If severe behavior occurs, then a more severe consequence can be used. For example, if students do not meet the group contingency criterion, then they work during the time they would have received the reward. However, if a severe misbehavior occurs (e.g., aggression, tantrum, severe noncompliance) and is rewarded by the group, then the group might miss recess or wait in their seats for 30 seconds after the bell rings.

STEP SIX

A feedback system that informs students how well they are doing on the target behavior is very important. A feedback system allows students to gauge their progress. It facilitates cooperation and competition between teams (to be discussed later). Simple visual feedback systems such as marks on the board, marbles in a jar, or happy or sad faces on a board are best. Even a tower of blocks that are colored in can be used. With the tower, a teacher colors in a block each time a student hands in an assignment or does the required number of problems. After a set number of blocks are completed, students are rewarded.

As part of the feedback system, it also helps to post the rules or the expected criterion in the classroom.

Troubleshooting Group Contingencies

There are a number of things that can go wrong with a group contingency. However, if a program is well-planned, then the difficulties are greatly reduced.

PROBLEM: *Student sabotage.*

> **Solution:** In some instances, one or two students may decide to sabotage the group contingency for the entire classroom. Although many teachers worry about this problem, it is relatively rare. The first thing to check if student sabotage occurs is to make sure the rewards that you have used are really valued and are effective reinforcers. Ask some of the students, and then talk with the offending student(s). If the problem continues, make the sabotaging student(s) a team all by themselves. In other words, have them work for their own contingency while the cooperating group continues to work for theirs.

PROBLEM: *Student failure.*

> **Solution:** If one student frequently fails to meet the contingency for the group but seems genuinely interested in cooperating, then the teacher should examine the criterion. It is foolish to set the criterion at 80% correct if one or two students are capable of only 60% accuracy at their current ability level. In this situation, the teacher should either: (1) Re-set the criterion for the whole group at a lower level, or (2) Keep the criterion at 80% for the group but set the level lower for the less capable students and slowly raise it as the students acquire the needed skills. The second option is preferred, particularly if the teacher does not highlight the fact that he/she has set a lower criterion for one or two students.

PROBLEM: *Failure after an initial success.*

> **Solution:** When this happens, it generally means two things: Either the consequences are not potent, or peer influence has increased. The teacher should check the reward and punishment components of the program. If intensified peer influence is suspected, the teacher may need to single out the most influential peers and: (1) Make them into confederates to help the program be a success, (2) Make them a special team and increase the privilege loss to this group, or (3) Call their parents into the classroom for a discussion. Oftentimes, consequences can be arranged at home for students.

PROBLEM: *The program has never really worked.*

> **Solution:** If this problem occurs, the teacher should again check the consequences of the program. If the consequences are appropriate, then the teacher should check the consistency of the program. The consistency of application by aides, volunteers, and assistants should also be checked. It is beneficial to have them help design the program and take a test over the rules to make sure each person understands the procedures. The target behaviors should be checked to see if they are specifically defined. The criterion should also be checked to determine if it is unrealistically high or if one or two students are not capable of meeting it.

PROBLEM: *Parents or principals argue that the program is unfair.*

> **Solution:** This occurs sometimes when parents and principals have not been adequately informed about the details of the program. Inform them and obtain their permission. If parents continue to be concerned, invite them to a meeting to discuss the issues and possibly modify the program.

If complaints only come from the students, tell them that they share responsibility with their peers and they need to help them. Also indicate that no threats or aggression will be tolerated. If students continue to complain, ignore the complainer and openly praise other cooperating students. When the complaining student demonstrates the desired behavior, specifically verbally reinforce him/her.

Ways to Enhance a Group Contingency

There are several ways to enhance the use of a group contingency. Some of these methods involve changing reinforcers, teams, the use of machines, and the use of specifically defined roles for students in the groups.

Teams

One of the most effective methods to improve a group contingency is to divide a classroom into teams. When used in classrooms, this procedure has been called the "Good Behavior Came" (Barrish, Saunders, & Wolf, 1969). Each team competes against itself as well as the other team. The group contingency should be designed so that: (1) Both teams can win, (2) Both teams can lose, and (3) One team can win and one team can lose. The best type of procedure to use is a group-all group contingency, with random selection of three unidentified students whose performance will be averaged to determine if the criterion is met for that team. The steps are:

STEP ONE

Divide a classroom into two separate teams—the composition should be decided by the teacher; each team should contain a mixture of poor, average, and above average students. Teams stay the same for one week, and they are reselected to form new teams the following week.

STEP TWO

Select the daily criterion (academic, behavior, or both). Post the criterion.

STEP THREE

Have students vote on a variety of rewards at the beginning of the week. Have one of these rewards available each day. It helps not to disclose the reward—use a grab bag or mystery motivator system.

STEP FOUR

At the end of the day, select at least two students' work from each team. Do not disclose their names, but average their performances to see if the criterion is matched or exceeded. If a behavior (e.g., talk-outs or out-of-seats) is being used with the group contingency, collect data on the students for each team. A clipboard is useful for making marks for each behavior.

STEP FIVE

If the team matches or exceeds the criterion, they are rewarded. If not, that team works on academics during the reward period.

STEP SIX

Prominently display how many times each team has met the criterion for each day of the week (this is a public posting procedure).

Variety In Reinforcement Procedures

Reinforcement is at the core of an effective group contingency system. Several ideas for reinforcement have already been presented in this module. In too many instances, group contingencies can be negatively focused. Although some punishment procedures may be necessary under some conditions, the positive aspects of a group contingency should be highlighted. Variety and anticipation of a reward for the group are excellent methods. The steps to enhance reinforcers are:

STEP ONE

Let students select reinforcers from a menu and vote on them. A reinforcement checklist can also be used, with students rating the reinforcers. The voting can then be used as a method to determine which reinforcers are the most potent (most votes) to the least potent (least votes). Use at least ten reinforcers that do not take too much time or cost too much money.

STEP TWO

If possible, display some of the reinforcers for the students. Let them see some of the items, pictures of activities, possible videos.

STEP THREE

Design a delivery system that maximizes variety and anticipation. Grab bags and mystery motivators have already been mentioned. Spinners and classroom bingo are also excellent systems.

Spinners

The spinner is simply a circle with unequal pie-shaped wedges and an arrow that can spin. Each numbered wedge represents a reinforcer. After the criterion is met, a selected student spins the arrow, and whatever wedge it lands on is the reinforcer for the group. The narrow wedges of the spinner should represent more expensive (time, effort, money) or valued reinforcers, while the larger wedges represent less expensive reinforcers (Jenson, Neville, Sloane, & Morgan, 1982).

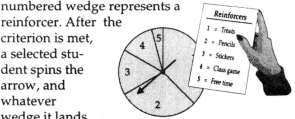

Reinforcers

1 = Treats
2 = Pencils
3 = Stickers
4 = Class game
5 = Free time

Classroom Bingo

This group contingency system requires a matrix of numbered squares (3 x 3-RED; 4 x 4-BLUE, 5 x 5-GREEN) that can be laminated on poster board and placed in the front of the classroom.

R	E	D
1	2	3
4	5	6
7	8	9

B	L	U	E
1	2	3	4
5	6	7	8
9	10	11	12
13	14	15	16

G	R	E	E	N
1	2	3	4	5
6	7	8	9	10
11	12	13	14	15
16	17	18	19	20
21	22	23	24	25

The teacher selects a reinforcer for the day and places it in front of the class near the matrix. Each time the group meets the criterion, a student is allowed to pull a number out of a bag. The number is marked on the matrix with a water-based marker. For the RED card, when the numbers selected form any row, column, or diagonal, the teacher gives the group the reinforcers. When the students as a group become proficient at reaching the criterion, the teacher can move to the BLUE card which requires four matches, and finally the GREEN card which requires five matches. This system is an excellent way to use a group contingency in which the teacher wants a criterion met several times a day or there may be several different criteria (e.g., 80% of homework completed and returned in the morning, no problems at recess, 80% of in-seat work completed that day, no more than one name on the board for classroom rule violations). It is also useful for slowly expanding the criterion requirement so that rewards can be given to the group less often for more work—first green, then blue, and then red.

Machines

The use of some types of machines and instruments can enhance the effectiveness of a group contingency. A stopwatch has been discussed earlier in this module. Similarly, a large classroom clock can be hooked up to a garage door opener. When the students are working, then the clock is running, accumulating free time for the students. However, when a student stops working or becomes disruptive, the teacher clicks the garage door opener and stops the clock until the student returns to work. The accumulated time on the big clock is the amount of free time for the group.

Another method of using a machine was devised by a high school math teacher, who brought a disc player to school that could be operated by remote control. Students were invited to bring their favorite discs to class to be played softly while students did independent seat work. If a student went off-task and stopped working, the teacher paused the disc for five minutes.

Student Administered Group Contingencies

This approach is one of the most promising for using a group contingency to improve academic skills. The procedure was developed by Wolfe, Fantuzzo, and Wolter (1984). The group contingency is based on teams made up of four members: a Coach, Scorekeeper, Referee, and Manager.

The **Coach** performs a self-instructional function for the group. He/she determines a daily academic goal and reminds the other team members of predetermined strategies for increasing their performance.

The **Scorekeeper** counts the number of correct academic responses made by the other team members, and calculates the total team score.

The **Referee** rechecks the Scorekeeper's work and acts as a built-in reliability check.

The **Manager** compares the daily score of the team to their self-determined goal and checks to see if the team has met the group contingency criterion for reinforcement. If they have, he/she declares they have won and arranges for the teacher to reinforce the group. The teacher sets a goal for the team to meet in order to be reinforced. It may take the team several days to be rewarded, depending on how high they set their goal and how hard they work.

The applied research on this type of approach with basic academic skills such as arithmetic performance has shown excellent results. It is particularly successful with unmotivated students who seem not to work for other incentives. Student-administered group contingencies could be enhanced by using some of the reward suggestions listed previously.

Case Study

Ms. Smith has had difficulty motivating several fourth grade students in her resource room to perform academically when they return to their regular class settings. The students work in the resource room but not in the regular classroom. Ms. Smith suspected that there might be peer pressure not to perform in front of other students. She decided to use a student-administered group contingency with a spinner reinforcer for the four students. All four boys were in the same regular classroom, and Ms. Smith explained the procedure to their teacher and gained his cooperation.

Initially, she had the students as a group select more than 20 rewards they would like, and she placed five on the spinner. She also made one of the most influential students, Tim, the Coach for the system. She taught Tim how to set a goal to meet the group contingency criterion. For example, when each of the four team members scored an average of 80% on the regular classroom arithmetic assignment for two days, then they were allowed to spin the spinner and receive a reward. She also taught Tim how to give a pep talk in the resource room about winning, and about the strategies for doing each problem, checking their answers, and not skipping any problems. She named one of the boys the Scorekeeper, and taught him to grade the papers at the end of day back in the resource room, with the help of the Referee. The Manager was taught to get the week's criterion from Ms. Smith (she would vary the criterion weekly from 75% to 90%) and how to calculate the average score. The Manager also publicly posted the team's daily effort on a large poster in the resource room.

The first week, the team took more than four days to get the 80% average. The next week, their average jumped to 95%, and Ms. Smith gave them the spinner and a bonus. She is also thinking of including a spelling test criterion for an additional spin.

References

Baer, G.C. & Richards, H.C. (1981). Moral reasoning and conduct problems in the classroom. _Journal of Educational Psychology, 73_(5), 664-670.

Barrish, H.H., Saunders, M., & Wolf, M.M. (1969). Good behavior game: Effects of individual contingencies for group consequences on disruptive behavior in a classroom. _Journal of Applied Behavior Analysis, 2_(2), 199-124.

Brown, D., Reschly, D., & Saber, D. (1974). Using group contingencies with punishment and positive reinforcement to modify aggressive behaviors in a head start classroom. _Psychological Record, 24_(4), 491-496.

Cowen, R.J., Jones, F.H., & Bellack, A.S. (1979). Grandma's rule with group contingencies: A cost-efficient means of classroom management. _Behavior Modification, 3_(3), 397-418.

Fishbein, J.E. & Wasik, B.H. (1981). Effect of the good behavior game on disruptive library behavior. _Journal of Applied Behavior Analysis, 14_(1), 89-93.

Greene, B.F., Bailey, J.S., & Barber, F. (1981). An analysis and reduction of disruptive behavior on school buses. _Journal of Applied Behavior Analysis, 14_(2), 177-192.

Jenson, W.R., Neville, M., Sloane, H.N., & Morgan, D.P. (1982). Spinners and chart moves: A contingency management system for school and home. _Child and Family Behavior Therapy, 4_, 83.

Salend, S.J. & Meddaugh, D. (1985). Using a peer-mediated extinction procedure to decrease obscene language. _Pointer, 30_(1), 8-11.

Speltz, M.L., Shimamura, J.W., & McReynolds, W.T. (1982). Procedural variations in group contingencies: Effects on children's academic and social behaviors. _Journal of Applied Behavior Analysis, 15_(4), 533-544.

Wolfe, J.A., Fantuzzo, J., & Wolter, C. (1984). Student-administered group-oriented contingencies: A method of combining group-oriented contingencies and self-directed behavior to increase academic productivity. _Child and Family Behavior Therapy, 6_(3), 45-60.

In-School Suspension Program

by *Ginger Rhode, Ph.D., Davis School District, Farmington, Utah*

Introduction

In-school suspension (ISS) is a disciplinary alternative to out-of-school suspension for less serious disciplinary infractions which do not pose a threat or danger to other persons, to the student him/herself, or to school/personal property (Stallworth, Frechtling, & Frankel, 1983). The literature concerning in-school suspension reflects a debate over whether the purpose of ISS should be to "punish" or to "counsel" the errant student (Garibaldi, 1979; Nielsen, 1979a). In this book, the primary purpose of ISS is to provide for continuity of a student's educational program while reducing the likelihood that the misbehavior will reoccur. It is not the intent of this book to describe an ISS program that will resolve all of a student's frustrations and problems, or eliminate his/her academic difficulties. ISS is just one component of a comprehensive school discipline and management system. It should be closely coordinated with the rest of the school's programs and resources (as well as community resources when appropriate), so that the end result will be a system which addresses the multiple needs of its students. Some of the issues involved in setting up an effective ISS program stem from confusion over

OBJECTIVES

By the end of this module, you will know:

- The purpose of ISS.
- The necessary conditions for an effective ISS program.
- How to organize an ISS program.
- Behaviors and contingencies for ISS programs.
- Procedural safeguards for implementing ISS.
- How to evaluate the effectiveness of ISS programs.

what the purpose of the program is and upon what principles of behavior it is based. This confusion is exemplified by programs which isolate ISS students from their peers and force them to work in restricted, supervised settings, but which have the intent of counseling these students toward more acceptable behavior. If the purpose of ISS is to reduce the probability that the misbehavior will reoccur, it is appropriate to refer for guidance to available research technology for reducing specific behaviors. Within this technology are several categories of interventions, all of which have numerous variations.

The behavior reductive technique which most closely resembles the intent and purpose of an ISS program is time-out, a powerful strategy when correctly implemented and when certain guidelines surrounding its use are followed. Confusion about what constitutes an effective ISS program may also stem partially from lack of understanding about the principles of behavior upon which time-out is based. Many of the components which are found within various ISS programs may not be inappropriate strategies for working with students who have problems; however, if they are part of the overall school management system, they should be in addition to, and outside of, the ISS program described in this module. Otherwise, the different strategies are likely to be in contradiction with one another, preventing the effective use of any of them. If ISS is to be viewed as a form of time-out, then the following information regarding the use of time-out is pertinent.

Time-Out

Time-out procedures, in the form of an in-school suspension program, serve as a behavior technique by denying a student (for a fixed period of time) the opportunity to receive the reinforcement available in the regular school setting. Time-out is actually time-out from positive reinforcement. ISS must actually provide for a situation which is not, in and of itself, reinforcing. Thus, an ISS program which isolates students but then provides an enjoyable, fun experience is not likely to be effective. For an ISS program to be effective, the following conditions must be present:

Conditions for an Effective ISS Program

1. An effective class- and school-wide discipline/management system must be in place.

2. Class/school rules must be specific, and must deal with observable and measurable behaviors. Students must know ahead of time exactly what the expectations are.

3. Rules should be publicly posted in classrooms and in areas of school-wide access (e.g., lunchrooms).

4. Teachers and administrators should follow a plan for positively reinforcing appropriate student behavior and performance. In other words, students should receive frequent (daily) positive recognition in some form for adhering to class and school expectations (e.g., a teacher may award the class a point every time the entire class arrives on time, and allow students to have a class party when they have accumulated a prespecified number of points). Positive consequences should outnumber negative ones at least 2:1. Thus, the "tone" of the school should be clearly positive.

   Unless the school provides positive reinforcement to students, no form of time-out will be effective! This cannot be stressed too strongly. Remember that time-out is time-out from a positive environment. Thus, while associating with their peers is reinforcing for most students, if classrooms or school are basically negative places to be, time-out will not work effectively. If ISS is more positively reinforcing than classrooms or school, time-out will not be effective either.

5. There should be a hierarchy of negative consequences on a class- and school-wide basis for students who choose to break the rules. These consequences do not need to be severe.

   In one junior high, the first instance of rule-breaking resulted in a warning, with the misbehaving student's name being placed on the chalkboard, while the second infraction resulted in the student having to remain for one minute after all the other students were dismissed from class. While this may not seem like a severe penalty, it did put enough distance between a student and his/her peers to serve as a deterrent to misbehavior.

In this same school, a third infraction resulted in 15 minutes of after-school detention; a fourth, in 30 minutes of after-school detention plus a call to the parent(s) and removal from class for the rest of the period. Time off-task and tardies were required to be made up in lunch detention and/or an after-school detention period. This was held every day for the 30-minute violations and for up to two hours twice each week for more serious infractions. In-school suspension in this school was used only when this hierarchy of negative consequences had been exhausted, or when the misbehavior was serious enough to warrant immediate removal from class.

In this junior high, students were kept in class to the extent that this was possible without compromising a conducive teaching/learning environment. Thus, ISS should be a last resort rather than a first resort. Following this type of approach to ISS as a component of a larger system also helps prevent overuse of the ISS setting.

6. There must be consistency and absolute follow through on all phases of a class/school management system, and including the ISS component. The strength of the total school program will come from the consistency and follow through in its use. Generally, this part of a program will depend upon administrator support, skill, and interest. However, a program can still be effective if an administrator will delegate responsibility for these areas and allow others to do this job (i.e., teachers with "career ladder" positions have sometimes served in this capacity with the express agreement of the building administrator).

   If students can avoid consequences they have earned, the entire program will be ineffective. If consistency and follow through are not present, one would do as well, or better, to do nothing at all.

7. There should be strong and continual communication and support among administration, faculty, counseling staff, special education personnel and the school team (psychologist, social worker) for the class/school management system. When all these personnel work together and support one another in using the system, it is not difficult to identify student problem areas which may require resources (e.g., social worker or counselor intervention)

> **The strength of the total school program will come from the consistency and follow through in its use.**

in addition to the negative consequences the student may have earned for misbehavior. In other words, the philosophy here is, "In this school we will help you solve the difficulties you may be having in school, and we will recognize those things you are doing well, but we expect you to follow the rules at all times, regardless." When there are strong ties, commitment, and a means of providing students with needed services within the school system as a whole, there is no need or reason for the ISS program.

Once all these conditions have been verified, an effective ISS program can be designed.

Organizing the ISS Program

Physical Location: Decide on a physical location for the ISS program. Schools usually utilize some variation of one of these types:

1. One type of location is an actual ISS room with student desks or study carrels. The size and type of room will usually depend upon what is available or may be made available in the school.

   a. Usually, a regular-size classroom will be sufficient for most programs. If there is a limited choice of classrooms, then the maximum number of students who can be served at any one time will be at least partially determined by the physical space available.

   b. Student desks should be placed to reduce student interaction (e.g., around the edges of the room facing away from each other, or even in traditional rows).

   c. The teacher's or supervisor's desk should be placed so that all students can be observed at all times. The back of the room is often a good place for the supervisor's desk.

2. An alternative type of program has been used successfully in several schools when there is no extra space in which to house the program, or when there are no funds to hire an outside supervisor.

   a. Special two-sided carrels are built from plywood. In two junior high schools, these were built in the shop class (supervised by the shop teachers) at least partly by students who were serving after-school detention time. The carrel is built of two pieces of plywood, each four feet wide and five feet high. The two sheets are hinged on one side with a piano hinge, and they have two removable braces, each with a groove within which the plywood fits. The carrel is large enough to conceal a student desk, and high enough so that when the student is seated at the desk, he/she cannot be seen from outside of the carrel, nor can he/she see anything outside of the carrel.

b. The carrel can be folded flat for storage when not in use, and can be moved to different locations as needed.

c. One or two of the carrels can be placed in or near the office area, if space permits and if visual stimuli can be limited. Very difficult students might be placed in these carrels.

d. The carrels are usually placed in classrooms near the office area (assuming office staff will be responsible for monitoring the students in the ISS carrels), typically in a corner at the back of the classroom. The piano hinge permits positioning of the carrel so that a student can gain easy entrance.

Personnel: In a separate ISS room, the supervisor(s) will usually be:

1. A full-time (or several part-time) certified teacher or other school professional whose only job is to supervise the ISS program.

2. Other trained professionals.

3. Teachers already employed in the school building who take turns supervising the program during their planning or consulting hours.

The first two options are possible when grants, alternative education funding, district or other funds are available. The third option has worked well in schools where no funding is available to hire supervision, and where teachers have been faced with the option of not having an ISS program unless they assist in the supervision. Some schools have even gone so far as to rule that only teachers who are willing to participate in the supervision may have students from their classrooms referred to the program!

When using a decentralized "carrel type" of program, with ISS students placed in classrooms, the personnel selection is of a different type. In this case, the following is pertinent:

1. Carrels are placed in classrooms that are located near the office of the program supervisor (administration, counseling staff, or other). Classrooms are selected on the basis of which teachers are willing to have an ISS carrel in their rooms, and which ones have good classroom management skills. In other words, the selected classrooms are run in an orderly fashion.

2. Classrooms for ISS carrel placement may be rotated over time.

3. Someone (administration, counseling staff, or other) must be responsible for the placement of the students, their continued monitoring (i.e., restroom breaks and lunch), the tracking of their assignments, and the amount of time made up.

Teachers in whose classrooms ISS carrels are placed are not in any way responsible for the ISS students who are making up time in their rooms. They merely agree to provide the space in which the ISS time may be made up, and to notify the office if there is any disruption or infraction of ISS rules. If this occurs, the student is removed to the office area to make up his/her time, the time to be made up is doubled, and parents are notified that a problem has occurred and what the options are for the student if it persists.

Immediacy of Placement: For ISS to serve as an effective behavior reducer, one must bear in mind that placing the student in the program immediately after the consequence has been earned is highly likely to maximize its effectiveness (Alberto & Troutman, 1982). Awareness of the relationship between immediacy and effectiveness is important, since available ISS literature suggests that this is rarely kept in mind (Nielsen, 1979a; Stallworth, et al., 1983; Winborne, 1980). Most schools appear to wait until the following day to begin an ISS assignment for a student. In addition to the question of effectiveness with delayed placement, one must consider that the student is free to continue to misbehave the rest of the current school day. Under such circumstances, it is possible that a student may believe that he/she has already "blown it," so why stop now?

Thus, it is recommended that the ISS user consider setting up the program so that students are placed as soon as possible after they have earned it. As long as there is an ISS supervisor who is monitoring beginning and ending times for individual students, this should not pose a problem.

Directly related to the issue of immediate placement is a "waiting list" for ISS. Some programs are set up to handle so few students, or have become so full, that students have a delay of days (or in one known case, weeks) before ISS time can begin. This is a totally ineffective use of ISS. If this type of situation arises, it is time to revise and adjust the rest of the school management program and the hierarchy of negative consequences. In addition, the school should increase positive consequences for appropriate behavior, so that fewer students will reach ISS.

If this area has already been examined and carefully adjusted, it may be necessary to increase the capacity of the ISS program. Length of stay in ISS should also be examined. School personnel may find that they get the same results with a one-day ISS assignment as with a three-day one. Likewise, a three-day placement may do as much to reduce misbehavior as a ten-day one. There may be instances for which half a day in ISS is sufficient; if the half day goes through the lunch period, even this can be a powerful consequence. The adage of not "resorting to surgery when a pill will do the trick" is an apt one here. The ISS user is advised to assign the least amount of time that is found to reduce reoccurrences of the misbehavior—with as little waiting to begin the time as possible. Not only does this make the job of supervision easier in terms of hours per student, but this keeps students where they should be—in the classroom as productive learners.

Informing Students of ISS Rules: Prior to beginning ISS, students should be informed of and should understand the behavior expectations while in ISS. Typical rules for ISS are simple:

1. No talking to other students.
2. No sleeping.
3. Stay in your seat.
4. Work on your schoolwork.

Rules should also be posted for students to see—on the wall of the ISS room or on the inside of an individual ISS carrel.

Students should be informed as to what will occur if they break ISS rules. Generally, it is appropriate to add one period (or 1 hour) to the student's total time for each rule infraction in a junior or senior high ISS program. At least one ISS program has added one full day to the student's time when a rule has been broken three or more times (Zimmerman & Archbold, 1979).

> The ISS user is advised to assign the least amount of time that is found to reduce reoccurrences of the misbehavior—with as little waiting to begin the time as possible.

If a student continues to break ISS rules, it would be appropriate to remove him/her from the ISS room (after only one disruption if he/she is in a classroom carrel), and to have time doubled and the parent(s) notified. If misbehavior continues, an out-of-school suspension and a parent conference may be appropriate.

Assignments During ISS: In the interest of continuity of the student's educational program, he/she should be required to complete classroom assignments as a condition of release from ISS when assigned time has been made up. If students are expected to do nothing for prolonged periods of assigned ISS time, further misbehavior may be encouraged. However, unless students find working on their school assignments so rewarding during ISS time that this time becomes viewed as positive by the student, problems arising from using ISS time in this fashion should be minimal.

There is evidence that students who are ISS candidates are likely to have academic difficulties to begin with, and denying them the opportunity to work on assignments during ISS time may increase the likelihood that the work will not be completed at all. If work is completed while in ISS, students will return to their classes with an increased probability of success, and will be prepared to participate in what is currently being taught. Parents are also likely to be supportive of an ISS program in which their children, some of whom may be poor students, are monitored on work completion.

Student Assignments: Several studies cite major problems with obtaining students' classroom assignments for them to work on during ISS (Chobot & Garibaldi, 1982; Nielsen, 1979a). This has been reported even when students have not begun ISS time until the following day. The problem has been reported largely as a teacher problem, in that teachers are sometimes unwilling to take the time to provide the assignments. One program, which did not have students begin assigned ISS time until the day after they had earned it, left the responsibility for gathering the assignments up to students. If they brought their assignments with them, they were released from ISS five minutes early. In-school suspension personnel reported that this worked well (Stallworth, et al., 1983).

Another junior high, which placed students in ISS as soon as they earned it, provided an office staff member (usually the person who had assigned the ISS time) to walk the student to his/her locker at that time to gather up all books, study materials, and assignments to which the student had access. In this school, the office kept a complete set of texts on hand to lend to students for ISS use when they reported they had left books at home, lent them to friends, or lost them.

In the same school, as one of the preliminary steps to having the student begin ISS, the person who assigned the time went through the student's class schedule one class at a time with him/her (after the walk to the locker) to determine for which classes he/she already had the assignments and materials and for which ones he/she did not. For each assignment needed, the student was asked to fill out a slip. As soon as these slips were filled out, they were delivered to the appropriate teachers by the student office aide. Teachers were expected to return the assignments to the office as soon as possible. In this school, most teachers wrote down the assignment during their next break between classes. Even if some teachers took longer to return assignments, getting one or two to begin with gave the student enough to work on until the others were sent back to the office.

In this school, responding to assignment requests was no problem for teachers. It is possible that cooperation occurred because administration expected it and told the teachers so. It was pointed out that these were their students, and that this was an opportunity to have assignment completion monitored (especially if the student completed assignments infrequently). Obviously, it is to the teachers' benefit to support an ISS program which is a part of student management for their classrooms and which assists in completion of assignments that they have given and view as meaningful.

If teacher cooperation is a problem, the administration may wish/need to adopt a policy whereby if an assignment is requested from a teacher and is not provided, the assignment will automatically be excused and will not count toward the student's grade. While this would be an extreme means of dealing with this problem, the presence of the policy would preclude its needing to be used very often.

Questions to Ask Before Implementing a School-Wide ISS Program

1. Have less punitive and less restrictive procedures/consequences been used for the student already?

2. Have the rules of appropriate behavior and the results for misbehavior been clearly explained and understood?

3. Are there procedures in place to fully explain rules of ISS behavior (and consequences for ISS infractions) to students so that these rules are completely understood?

4. Have district regulations concerning the use of an ISS program been reviewed and complied with? Has district support for the program been obtained?

5. Are there plans in place in classes/school to ensure that appropriate student behavior is recognized and reinforced (at a minimum 2:1 ratio), and is school basically a positive place for students to be?

6. Has the ISS program been organized so as to provide follow-up to assignment there? In other words, do students who are assigned to the program show up? What will occur (every time) if students do not show up? Are students aware of what will happen if they don't show up?

Common Behaviors for Which ISS May be Used, and Suggested Consequences

For fighting, teacher defiance, arguing, name-calling, or destruction of school/personal property, immediate removal from the classroom and placement in ISS is warranted. For the first offense of any of these, one full day in ISS is suggested. A second offense would result in a two-day ISS assignment; a third in a three-day assignment plus a parent conference to resolve the problem. At the parent conference, further action by the school would be defined should the problem reoccur. Any other school personnel who might be relevant to resolving the problem would also be invited to the meeting. Action by the school might take the form of a student contract, a referral to special education, assignment to a social skills or problem-solving group offered through the counseling staff, or out-of-school suspension.

For failing to report for a two-hour after-school detention, a half-day ISS assignment through the lunch period would be appropriate. This assignment would be based on the rule that any assigned time that is missed will automatically double. For repeated truancy or tardiness that adds up to 15 minutes or more of cumulative time missed from school, it is suggested that after-school detention time equalling the amount of time for unexcused truancy/tardiness be assigned before resorting to ISS. In other words, if a student cuts two class periods, he/she would be assigned to a two-hour after-school detention (called "eighth period" in some schools). If he/she missed half a day of school, two of these after-school detentions would be assigned, etc. Assigning after-school detention as a first course of action helps keep students in class if they have already been truant; most can ill afford further loss of class time. If students are truant again before assigned time has been made up, or if they have not shown up for an after-school detention (assigned time doubled as a result and the student still did not show up), only then would the total time owed convert to ISS time.

Preventing students from missing assigned after-school detention is one means of avoiding unnecessary ISS time. Good parent communication is one way to achieve this. For students who have previously missed after-school detention time, parents can be told to expect a note that has been signed by the after-school detention supervisor, indicating that time has been made up. Parents are asked for support and assistance when notes are not brought home. Repeat nonattenders can also be escorted from their last class period of the day to after-school detention by a staff member. This will help avoid conversion of detention time to ISS time and will prevent the student from escaping consequences he/she has earned.

It is suggested that for tardies (up to 15 minutes each), the following guidelines be considered:

Tardies per Class	Consequences
1-2	none
3	1 lunch detention + call parent (tell that student has 3 and what will happen with a 4th)
4	30 minutes after-school detention + *U* in citizenship for class + call parent(s)
5-6	1 hour after-school detention + call parent(s)
7-8	2 hours after-school detention + call parent(s)
9	ISS + parent conference

For tardies of 15 minutes and longer, the rule of assigning make-up time after school equal to the amount of missed time is suggested.

Legal Issues and Cautions

1. Use of ISS, as with all components of the school management system, should follow due process procedures (including any district guidelines/policies).

   a. Students must know ahead of time what the rules are and what will happen if they break them.

   b. When students are accused of breaking the rules, they must be given the opportunity to respond to the accusations.

   c. Parents must be notified that some action is being taken.

2. Parents and community members should be informed of the total school management system ahead of time. This can be accomplished in many ways: a presentation given on Back-to-School Night, a meeting sponsored by the PTA, written information to parents included with registration materials or with the school calendar, or in a school handbook. Parents should be encouraged to ask questions and voice concerns before problems arise.

3. Support of school board members and district supervisors should be obtained ahead of time for all components of the school management system, including ISS. They should be invited to the school to see what is proposed and discuss the program. Differences which they believe are too great for them to support must be resolved before the program is initiated. The program must have full support from these individuals to avoid future problems (e.g., a parent disagrees with the school's program and

refuses to allow his/her child to have consequences which have been earned).

4. Length of assigned time in ISS should not be excessive and should bear a relationship to the severity of the student's infraction. Assigned time should be that of a least restrictive model, with less stringent procedures such as after-school detention and lunch detention being used first.

5. Assigning negative consequences should not be confused with denying a student his/her basic rights. For example, it is probably illegal to deny a student access to the restroom, the telephone, or his/her lunch.

Evaluating the Effectiveness of an ISS Program

The ISS program is meeting its objective if: (1) The misbehavior which resulted in students being assigned to ISS decreases overall in the school and/or is not repeated by the students who have spent time in ISS; and, (2) If students make up assignments they have missed while in ISS. Evaluation of program effectiveness has been weak or absent in most available ISS research.

Ideally, comparable information from previous years should be examined:

1. How many students were suspended out-of-school in previous years?

2. How many total days of out-of-school suspension were assigned in previous years?

3. What was the frequency for each type of behavior problem reported in previous years (i.e. fights, truancy/tardiness, teacher defiance, property destruction)?

4. How many students spent time in in-school suspension in previous years?

5. How many total days of in-school suspension were assigned in previous years?

   If no information is available for the previous years, comparisons are difficult.

   To make comparisons of program effectiveness, the information listed here would be collected during the current school year. In addition to making comparisons in each of these areas, out-of-school and in-school

suspension totals for each year should be compared.

The program can be considered to be losing ground when out-of-school suspensions, in-school suspensions, or a total of the two for a given year (in terms of number of suspensions or total number of assigned days) increase. No change would be indicated when these figures remain essentially the same. Positive progress would be noted when the totals in any of these categories decrease, or when the total number of days assigned decreases (even if the number of suspensions remains the same). All of these comparisons would be made assuming a school population which remains about the same size. If significant changes occur in the number of students enrolled for different years, adjustments need to be made in the comparisons to allow for this.

In addition, the following questions should be asked and responses tallied to determine satisfaction with the program:

1. Are teachers and parents satisfied with the results of the ISS program? Do they view it as an effective deterrent to misbehavior?

2. How do teachers rate overall student behavior in the classrooms and in the school as a whole?

3. Do teachers see any areas needing improvement in the overall school management system?

4. Do students, parents, and teachers view the implementation and the procedures of the ISS program as fair?

Answers to these questions and a review of information collected from past and current years will give direction for the next year's program. This same information can be compiled and examined for each term, so that needed adjustments can be made during the school year as well.

Applications to Other Programs

The ISS program which has been described is a basic program for use in a regular junior or senior high school. An ISS component can also be effective with other populations/programs. Some of these are described following:

Resource (Special Education) Program: The use of ISS can be a very effective component of a resource student's program for reducing misbehavior. Usually the program would be used for this student in exactly the same way that it is used for the rest of the school.

Some resource teachers like to have their own ISS carrel(s) in their classroom for students who are in the program. Because some resource students may have gained a lot of attention from teachers and peers for disruptive, acting-out behavior in the past, denying them this attention through the use of ISS in the resource or other room offers one alternative for reducing these behaviors.

Integrating the use of the regular school ISS program (or a similar use of one within the resource program) can also be useful in mainstreaming students back to regular classes. Consistency and coordination between the resource and regular school programs will make both more effective for the resource student by providing common expectations and consequences for both settings.

Self-Contained (Special Education) Program: A student in a self-contained special education program would not be expected to make use of the regular school ISS program, although the availability of such a program is useful when he/she is mainstreamed back to a regular program. A student whose needs have been severe enough to warrant placement in a self-contained program would, in most cases, require closer monitoring than the regular program can provide. A lower pupil-teacher ratio would also be desirable in order to carry out a program as intensive as may be needed by these students. In most cases, the self-contained form of ISS would be the use of a type of time-out:

1. **Nonseclusionary Time-Out**—student is not removed from the instructional setting; rather, the teacher denies the student access to positive reinforcement through a manipulation of the environment, which signals a period of time during which access is denied (e.g., student places head down on desk or teacher turns out lights for a period of time). This type is appropriate for a generalized minor disturbance.

2. **Exclusionary Time-Out**—student is removed from the instructional setting to another part of the classroom as a means of denying access to positive reinforcement (e.g., removed to a chair facing a corner or placed in a screened-off area of the room).

3. **Seclusionary Time-Out**—use is made of a "time-out room" to which the student is removed. This room is available for total social isolation, and results in the denial of access to any and all potential reinforcement from the teacher, classmates, or classroom environment. For self-contained populations, time-out can be a very powerful behavior reduction technique. Before utilizing time-out in any form as part of a program for a self-contained population, the reader is advised to become familiar with time-out procedures to assure proper use of the technique and to avoid serious legal implications.

Elementary School Use of ISS: In-school suspension can be a very useful tool in an elementary school for dealing with the most serious behaviors this population presents. It is expected that an ISS program in an elementary school can all but replace out-of-school suspensions. Guidelines and cautions for using ISS at the elementary level are similar to those with older students. The main difference is in the area of length of time assigned for offenses (see Table following).

> The key to a successful elementary ISS program is to deny students an "audience" for their misbehavior.

Generally, elementary ISS programs are decentralized, with students who have earned ISS time spending it in classrooms other than their own. In an elementary school utilizing this type of ISS system, the principal needs to secure cooperation from teachers to provide a desk and chair in an isolated part of their classrooms. The principal may then assign students to complete ISS time at the designated space in any classroom in the school. The principal is the only person who will assign students ISS time; the classroom teacher provides the space only and reports any ISS rule infractions to the office immediately, either by intercom or a note sent with a student. The principal, or a designee, is responsible for distributing and collecting ISS assignments, and for coordinating restroom breaks and lunch. The key to a successful elementary ISS program is to deny students an "audience" for their misbehavior. This is accomplished by cross-grading ISS placements. Thus, a sixth grade student might be assigned ISS time in a kindergarten or first grade classroom, and

Behaviors for Which ISS May Be Assigned	Length of Assigned Time
Fighting, Severe Disruption (e.g., throw desk or chair)	*First offense:* Grades 1-3 — 30 minute ISS + miss next recess + notify parent Grades 4-6 — 1 ISS + miss all recesses + notify parent *Second offense:* Grades 1-3 — 1 hour ISS + miss all recesses that day + notify parent Grades 4-6 — 3 hours ISS + miss remaining recesses + notify parent *Third offense:* Grades 1-3 — 3 hours ISS + miss remaining recesses + notify parent Grades 4-6 — all day ISS + notify parent *Fourth offense:* Grades 1-6 — ISS until parent conference held
Back-Talk to Teacher (argue, call a name); Teacher Defiance	Same consequences as for fighting, with the addition of: *First and second offense:* Grades 1-3 — verbal apology to teacher Grades 4-6 — written apology to teacher *Third offense:* Grades 1-6 — written apology to teacher, verbal apology to entire class
Destruction of Property	Same consequences as for fighting with the addition of restitution of property or clean-up within the school, as appropriate.
Student has had 4 rule infractions in class in one day	Grades 1-6 — 30 minutes ISS + notify parent
Student has had 5 rule infractions in class in one day	Grades 1-6 — 1 hour ISS + notify parent
Student has had 6 rule infractions in class in one day	Grades 1-6 — ISS rest of day + parent conference

vice-versa. Students who are assigned to ISS more than three times are candidates for additional intervention. The principal would call a conference with the classroom teacher, counselor, and parent(s) to discuss the problems. Other school personnel (psychologist, social worker) would be invited to the conference as judged necessary.

A student contract which would go home to the parent(s) on a daily basis (with built-in rewards and penalties at home), referral to social skills training groups, or referral to special education would all be considered as possible solutions. A trial period for the additional intervention would be defined, with review by the same group. Interventions would be revised, strengthened, or discontinued as this group recommended for managing student behavior.

References

Alberto, P.A. & Troutman, A.C. (1982). *Applied behavior analysis for teachers*. Columbus, OH: Charles E. Merrill.

Chobot, R.B. & Garibaldi, A. (1982). In-school alternatives to suspension: A description of ten school district programs. *The Urban Review, 14*(4), 317-336.

Garibaldi, A.M. (1979). In-school alternatives to suspension: Trendy educational innovations. *The Urban Review, 11*(2), 97-103.

Nielsen, L. (1979a). Successful in-school suspension programs: The counselor's role. *The School Counselor, 26*(5), 325-333.

Stallworth, W.L., Frechtling, J.A., & Frankel, M. (1983). In-school suspensions: A pilot program. *Spectrum, 1*(1), 23- 31.

Winborne, C.R. (1980). In-school suspension programs: The King William County model. *Educational Leadership, 37*(6), 466- 469.

Zimmerman, J. & Archbold, L.A. (1979). On campus suspension: What it is and why it works. *NASSP Bulletin, 63*(428), 63-67.

Recommended Resources

Bass, A. (1980). Another approach to suspension. *NASSP Bulletin, 64*(436),109-110.

Brookover, W., Beamer, L., Efthim, H., Hathaway, D., Lezotte, L., Miller, S., Passalacqua, J., Tornatzky, L. (1982). *Creating effective schools: An in-service program for enhancing school learning climate and achievement.* Holmes Beach, FL: Learning Publications.

Chizak, L. (1984). We use a detention room to keep kids' behavior problems in check. *American School Board Journal, 171*(7), 29-30.

Copeland, M. (1985). *In-school suspension: From values clarification to the breakfast club.* Unpublished manuscript, University of Utah.

Corbett, A.H. (1981). Is your I.S.S. program meeting its goals? Take a closer look. *NASSP Bulletin, 65*(448), 59-63.

Frith, G.H., Lindsey, J.D., & Sasser, J.L. (1980). An alternative approach to school suspension: The dothan model. *Phi Delta Kappan, 61*(9), 637-638.

Keifer, D.A. (1980). An inexpensive alternative to suspension. *NASSP Bulletin, 64*(434), 112-114.

Mizell, M.H. (1978). Designing and implementing effective in-school alternatives to suspension. *The Urban Review, 10*(3), 213-226.

Nielsen, L. (1979b). Let's suspend suspensions: Consequences and alternatives. *Personnel and Guidance Journal, 57*(9), 442-445.

Sweeney-Rader, J., Snyder, G.L., Goldstein, H., & Rosenwald, P. (1980). School suspensions: An in-house prevention model. *Children Today, 9*(2), 19-21.

Weiss, K. (1983). In-school suspension: Time to work, not socialize. *NASSP Bulletin, 67*(464), 132-133.

Peer Tutoring

by Susan L. Fister, M.Ed., Education 1st, Salt Lake City, Utah

Introduction

Peer tutoring is defined as a one-to-one teaching arrangement in which peers serve as instructional agents/facilitators for one another in an academic setting. Instruction can be focused on academic and/or social skills, and can be applied across a variety of instructional settings. Peers can serve as both tutors and tutees in diverse subject areas and with a wide range of student age and ability levels. Students can serve as monitors for other students, can reinforce teacher directed instruction, or can provide a format for structured practice or review activities. This intervention can be applied in general education settings as a class-wide strategy, or as a remedial strategy in special education settings. Additionally, students with unique social and academic skill deficits can be integrated with other students in a peer tutoring capacity. It is important to broadly define the range of peer tutoring applications and structures in order to maintain creativity and flexibility in its use.

Types of Peer Tutoring Systems

There are at least five major types of peer tutoring structures that are being used in schools today. The most common forms of peer tutoring are listed below. Frequently, teachers will combine elements of

OBJECTIVES

By the end of this module, you will know:
- What class-wide peer tutoring is.
- What makes peer tutoring effective.
- How to implement a class-wide peer tutoring system.
- Cautions regarding peer tutoring.

different peer tutoring structures or will integrate other instructional strategies with peer tutoring (e.g., study guides, graphic organizers, management systems) to improve academic achievement and motivation.

1. "Traditional" Peer Tutoring
2. Cross-Age Tutoring (Scruggs et al., 1985)
3. Reverse Role Tutoring (Top & Osguthorpe, 1987)
4. Class-Wide Peer Tutoring (Delquadri, Greenwood, Whorton, Carta, & Hall, 1986)
5. Class-Wide Student Tutoring Teams (Maheady, Harper, & Sacca, 1990)

Is Peer Tutoring Effective?

Peer tutoring procedures have proven effective in increasing students' academic skills, as well as their social skill competence, self-confidence, and friendship skills. A variety of studies have shown that both tutors and tutees showed improvement in achievement (Heward, Heron, & Cooke, 1982; Harris & Sherman, 1973), not only in terms of accuracy of responses, but also in the rate of completion. Class-wide peer tutoring systems have demonstrated higher scores on weekly tests and higher levels of academic responding (Greenwood, et al., 1984). An increase in opportunities for academic responding increases achievement, and also tends to decrease disruptive behavior (McKenzie & Budd, 1981). The results from an extensive class-wide peer tutoring project which involved 22 teachers and 571 students (47 of whom were either receiving special education services or were identified as at-risk by their classroom teachers) indicated that both correct and incorrect rates of performance significantly improved for the overall group (Lovitt, Fister, Kemp, Moore, & Schroeder, 1992).

Long-term effects of peer tutoring have been studied for two years, and suggest that academic gains continue to persist and consumer satisfaction remains from moderate to high over this time period (Greenwood, et al., 1987). Furthermore, both high- and low-achieving students benefit from peer tutoring, showing increases in on-task performance, "participation, and practice for all children, even those most delayed or most difficult to motivate" (Carta,

> Class-wide systems can help to integrate students into the entire classroom routine without unnecessarily singling out or labeling students for special assignments.

Greenwood, Dinwiddie, Kohler, & Delquadri, 1987, p. 1). Class-wide systems can help to integrate students into the entire classroom routine without unnecessarily singling out or labeling students for special assignments. Even unmotivated students may become more involved with peers in the classroom learning process.

Advantages to Peer Tutoring

1. **Creates a more desirable pupil/teacher ratio**: A one-on-one teaching situation can provide for closer monitoring and feedback. Students can be taught to catch 96% of other students' errors!

2. **Increases students' time on-task**: Performing in front of another student and monitoring another student's responses increases the engaged time.

3. **Provides more opportunities to respond**: Increased opportunities to respond correlates positively with higher student achievement.

4. **Increases opportunity for and immediacy of error correction**: One-on-one instruction can allow for closer monitoring of student responses and for the use an effective error correction procedure.

5. **Enhances student motivation**: Peer tutoring provides an alternative instructional arrangement to the more common lecture or "do it yourself." Motivational systems can be employed to create a game format.

6. **Increases opportunity to receive positive feedback**: When students respond correctly, they are given specific and descriptive feedback, positive praise, and encouragement.

7. **Provides a forum for practicing and reinforcing interpersonal/social skills**: Pairing students together can create opportunities for positive role modeling, problem solving, and more appropriate interactions among students.

Disadvantages to Peer Tutoring

1. **Increased time demands (initially)**: Instructional time will need to be devoted to proper peer training and to procedures for ongoing monitoring of student performance.

2. **Increased noise levels**: Guidelines, rules, and procedures for noise reduction will need to be

taught and reinforced to create a manageable learning environment.

3. **Student bickering and complaining**: This is common when students are placed in heterogeneous groups. Procedures will need to be in place to promote appropriate social behavior.

4. **Point Inflation**: Rules and rewards will need to be in place to discourage cheating while encouraging accurate counting and recording of points earned during tutoring sessions.

5. **Ethical Concerns**: Proper and effective training of tutors is required. Careful consideration should be given in matching students for tutoring dyads. It is also a good idea to inform parents of the benefits of peer tutoring.

Implementing Class-Wide Peer Tutoring

1. **Divide class into two teams.** Students can be randomly assigned to teams, or the teacher may want to make team assignments in order to ensure equitable teams. Teams may be given a name, number, color, etc.

2. **Assign students to dyads (tutoring pairs).** Students can be randomly assigned to dyads, or the teacher may want to make dyad assignments in order to accommodate individual differences. Teach a procedure to be used when one partner is absent. For example, students can rotate tutoring in a group of three, and then one of the scores can be doubled.

3. **Train dyads to conduct tutoring sessions.** Carefully demonstrate and model the tutoring process for students. A tutoring procedure like the one illustrated in the diagram can be used while training students how to conduct tutoring sessions. Students should also be taught to use a scorecard like the one pictured at the end of this module to keep track of correct and erroneous responses. The scorecard should also provide a space for points, which are awarded for correct performance. Examples of behaviors for earning bonus points are listed on the card. The teacher will move throughout the classroom during the tutoring sessions and provide specific and descriptive praise for the correct use of the tutoring procedures and appropriate social behaviors. Bonus points are recorded on the dyads' scorecards to help reinforce the procedures. A sufficient amount of

guided practice should be provided so that students are firm on the procedure. Students will then switch tutoring roles after ten to 15 minutes. Bonus points are again awarded during the second tutoring session.

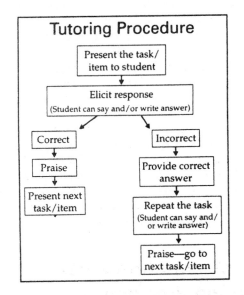

4. **Total the points from the tutoring session.** The two students in each dyad will add their tutoring points together for a daily total. This total should also include any bonus points that were earned by each partner during the tutoring session.

5. **Post the daily point totals on a game chart.** The total score for each dyad is then publicly posted on a game chart/team score sheet similar to the one shown at the end of this module. Since dyad scores are reported as a total number, there is no identification of individual student scores, and no embrarrassment. Dyads work cooperatively, earning combined points.

6. **Select a winning team each day and week.** All dyad scores from each team are totaled each day to determine a daily winning team. At the end of the week, daily totals are tabulated to determine the winning team of the week. Smaller rewards can be given to daily winning teams, and a grand prize can be awarded to the winning team of the week. Some ideas for recognizing teams include: posting results in the classroom and on the school bulletin board, printing results in a school bulletin or newsletter, achievement certificates, raffle drawings, no-homework passes, half-homework passes, erase a grade, extra credit, positive note home, elevate a grade, procrastination passes, free-time minutes, music, snacks, etc.

7. **Regularly assess individual student performance on material related to tutoring tasks.** Quizzes or some other type of assessment should be administered individually and at least weekly to determine student growth on the objectives which are being practiced and reinforced through the tutoring sessions. Individual accountability is necessary in order to make future instructional decisions regarding the needs of each student, as well as to determine the effectiveness of the tutoring sessions. Quizzes are administered individually and can be recorded individually by the teacher. However, a dyad quiz score can be reported as a total and recorded as a daily entry on the team score sheet. In some classrooms, teachers conduct class-wide peer tutoring on Monday, Wednesday, and Friday, and administer quizzes on Tuesday and Thursday.

Troubleshooting a Peer Tutoring Program

Most problems with peer tutoring occur when dyads refuse to work, or stray off-task. Some ways to deal with this are discussed here.

PROBLEM: *Students are not working together in a pleasant and efficient manner.*

Solution: Increase your use of effective praise by finding things that the tutoring dyads are doing right. For example, when you catch the tutee or tutor engaged in the appropriate behaviors, move in next to the student(s), place yourself at their eye level, look at the student(s), and in a calm, pleasant voice and with a pleasant facial expression, say something like, "Nice job, you are dictating the items clearly, giving your partner an appropriate correction, giving your partner immediate feedback when they are correct, moving through the items quickly, speaking in an appropriate voice tone," etc.

PROBLEM: *A student is becoming frustrated, even when given lots of positive feedback.*

Solution: Check the difficulty of the assignment. If the student is making too many errors, the task may need to be modified or more teacher-directed instruction may need to occur.

PROBLEM: *One or two dyads tend to behave inappropriately during peer tutoring.*

Solution: Remind the students of the final rewards. Smaller rewards, like additional recess, stickers, etc., can be given to dyads for improvement in daily totals. Rewards can also be given for team daily totals and for the winning team of the week. If problems persist or are being reinforced by other students in the class, special class-wide rewards may be established. For example, when troublesome dyads follow the prescribed behavioral expectations, they may earn additional bonus points for their entire team.

PROBLEM: *One of the dyads seems to take much longer than the others to finish their work.*

Solution: Set time limits on how much more work needs to be accomplished within the next five minutes, before being excused, etc. Place timers on the dyads' tables and establish a number of items that needs to be completed before the bell rings.

PROBLEM: *Students are not following the established rules; this results in chaos and confusion.*

Solution: Teach students the behavioral expectations that will be in effect during class-wide peer tutoring. This should include appropriate voice tone and level, materials necessary, seating arrangement, clear procedures for administering items, correcting errors, and providing positive feedback to partners, along with procedures for handling complaints, disagreements, etc. Each student should be able to articulate these procedures. Students should also be clear on the procedures which will be used if partners choose not to follow the behavioral expectations. In chronic or severe cases, penalties or other strategies may need to be used.

PROBLEM: *The system was working well, but now one or two dyads are having difficulty.*

Solution: Schedule meetings with dyads and/or provide weekly opportunities for dyads and teams to give feedback on the tutoring sessions. This can be handled by written or verbal processing and can offer opportunities for tutors to share their experiences, offer helpful suggestions to each other, and find solutions for any difficulties. This will offer opportunities to provide feedback to the dyads without singling any of them out. The teacher may want to structure a few open-ended questions for dyads to respond to on a weekly basis.

PROBLEM: *One dyad has particularly high scores for tutoring, but they struggle on mastery tests.*

Solution: This may indicate that students are cheating. Implement surprise daily checking to prevent cheating and point inflation. Randomly select and check one paper each day to reinforce accurate counting and totaling of points.

PROBLEM: *A couple of students are assigned to dyads with people that they don't get along with; there is some quarreling within the dyads.*

Solution: Inform students that dyads and their team structures will only stay in place for one or two weeks. Teach students that bickering and complaining are unacceptable. Ignore complaints and bickering. If problems arise with the dyads, they should be encouraged to resolve their own difficulties. Reinforce cooperative working groups. In rare circumstances, it may be necessary to change the tutor-tutee pairs.

Cautions

1. Be sure that thorough teacher training and modeling of the class-wide peer tutoring procedures have occurred. Students need several practice opportunities with close supervision, monitoring, and feedback in order to become skilled at the procedures. Post and review rules. Reinforce those students/dyads who comply with the rules.

2. Class-wide peer tutoring is designed as a motivational, guided practice activity to allow students multiple opportunities to practice academic and social behavior with feedback. Do not allow students to use punishment.

References

Carta, J., Greenwood, C.R., Dinwiddie, G., Kohler, F., & Delquadri, J. (1987). *The Juniper Gardens classwide peer tutoring programs for spelling, reading, and math: Teacher's manual*. Kansas City, KS: University of Kansas.

Delquadri, J., Greenwood, C.R., Whorton, D., Carta, J., & Hall, R.V. (1986). Classwide peer tutoring. *Exceptional Children, 52*, 535-542.

Greenwood, C.R., Kohler, F.C., Dinwiddie, G., Bailey, V., Carta, J., Dorsey, D., Nelson, C., Rotholz, D., & Shulte, D. (1987). Field replication of classwide peer tutoring. *Journal of Applied Behavior Analysis, 20*, 151-160.

Greenwood, C.R., Dinwiddie, G., Terry, B., Wade, L., Stanley, S., Thibadeau, S., & Delquadri, J. (1984). Teacher-versus peer-mediated instruction: An ecobehavioral analysis of achievement outcomes. *Journal of Applied Behavior Analysis, 17*, 521-538.

Harris, V.W. & Sherman, J. (1973). Effects of peer tutoring and consequences on the math performance of elementary classroom students. *Journal of Applied Behavior Analysis, 6*, 587-597.

Heward, W., Heron, T., & Cooke, N. (1982). Tutor huddle: Key element in a classwide peer tutoring system. *The Elementary School Journal, 83*, 115-123.

Lovitt, T., Fister, S., Kemp, K., Moore, R.C., & Schroeder, B.E. (1992). *Translating research into practice (TRIP): Teaching strategies*. Longmont, CO: Sopris West.

Maheady, L. Harper, G.F., & Sacca, M.K. (1990). *Heads together: A peer-mediated option for improving the academic achievement of heterogeneous learning groups*. Manuscript submitted for publication.

McKenzie, M.L. & Budd, K.S. (1981). A peer tutoring package to increase mathematics performance: Examination of generalized exchanges in classroom behavior. *Education & Treatment of Children, 4*(1), 1-15.

Scruggs, T.E. & Osguthorpe, R.T. (1986). Tutoring interventions within special education settings: A comparison of cross-age and peer tutoring. *Psychology in the Schools, 23*, 187-193.

Top, B.L. & Osguthorpe, R.T. (1987). Reverse-role tutoring: The effects of handicapped students tutoring regular class students. *The Elementary School Journal, 87*, 413-423.

Recommended Resources

Bailey, J.S., Timbers, G.D., Phillips, E.L., & Wolf, M.M. (1971). Modification of articulation errors of predelinquents by their peers. *Journal of Applied Behavior Analysis, 46,* 265-281.

Bar-Eli, N. & Raviv, A. (1982). Underachievers as students. *Journal of Educational Research, 75,* 139-143.

Carnine, D.W. (1976). Effects of two teacher-presentation rates on off-task behavior, answering correctly, and participation. *Journal of Applied Behavior Analysis, 9,* 199-206.

Cloward, R.D. (1967). Studies on tutoring. *Journal of Experimental Education, 36,* 14-25.

Cohen, J. (1986). Theoretical considerations of peer tutoring. *Psychology in the Schools, 23,* 175-186.

Csapo, M. (1972). Peer models reverse the "one bad apple spoils the barrel" theory. *Teaching Exceptional Children, 5,* 20-24.

Ehly, S. (1986). *Peer tutoring: A guide for school psychologists.* Washington, DC: National Association of School Psychologists.

Johnson, M. & Bailey, J.S. (1974). Cross-age tutoring: Fifth graders as arithmetic tutors for kindergarten children. *Journal of Applied Behavior Analysis, 7,* 223-232.

Killoran, J., Allred, J., Striefel, S., & Quintero, M. (1987). *The mainstreaming teacher's guide to designing and implementing a peer tutoring system.* Logan, UT: VSSM Peer Tutoring Program, Utah State University.

Koskinen, P.S. & Wilson, R.M. (1982). *Developing a successful tutoring program.* New York: Teachers College Press.

Limbrick, E., McNaughton, S., & Glynn, T. (1985). Reading gains for underachieving tutors and tutees in a cross-age tutoring program. *Journal of Child Psychology and Psychiatry, 6,* 939-953.

Maher, C.A. (1982). Behavioral effects of using conduct problem adolescents as cross-age tutors. *Psychology in the Schools, 19,* 360-364.

Pierce, M.M., Stahlbrand, K., & Armstrong, S.B. (1984). *Increasing student productivity through peer tutoring programs.* Austin, TX: Pro-Ed.

Pigott, H.E., Fantuzzo, J.W., & Clement, P.W. (1986). The effects of reciprocal peer tutoring and group contingencies on the academic performance of elementary school children. *Journal of Applied Behavior Analysis, 19,* 93-98.

Strain, P.S., Cooke, T.P., & Apolloni, T. (1976). The role of peers in modifying classmates' social behavior: A review. *Journal of Special Education, 10,* 351-356.

Strain, P.S., Shores, R.E., & Timm, M.A. (1977). Effects of peer social initiations on the behavior of withdrawn preschool children. *Journal of Applied Behavior Analysis, 10,* 289-298.

Trovato, J. & Bucher, B. (1980). Peer tutoring with or without home-based reinforcement for reading remediation. *Journal of Applied Behavior Analysis, 13,* 129-141.

Yogev, A. & Ronen, R. (1982). Cross-age tutoring: Effect on tutors' attributes. *Journal of Educational Research, 75,* 261-268.

Dyad Scorecard

Tutee _____   Tutor _____

Date _____   Task _____

Bonus Points _____   Total Points _____

Item #	Correct (+)	Incorrect (−)	Used Correction Procedure
1. _____			_____
2. _____			_____
3. _____			_____
4. _____			_____
5. _____			_____
6. _____			_____
7. _____			_____
8. _____			_____

Bonus Point Behaviors

- Use of praise
- Use of correction procedure
- Accurate use of scorecard
- Clearly presenting items

Team Score Sheet

Team # [ ] **Weekly Total** [ ]

Dyads	Monday	Tuesday	Wednesday	Thursday	Friday
#1					
#2					
#3					
#4					
#5					
#6					
#7					
#8					
Daily Totals					

Self-Recording to Enhance Performance

by William R. Jenson, Ph.D., University of
Utah, and H. Kenton Reavis, Ed.D., Utah
State Office of Education

Introduction

To keep careful track of ourselves on a daily basis,
we self-record our behavior. For example, many of
us collect data about our weight first thing in the
morning. Other people collect data on how many
miles they jog, while others record how much money
they have spent in their checking account. Simply
stated, self-recording is the systematic collection of
data on oneself. However, self-recording is more
than just casually observing one's own behavior. It
actually involves: (1) **Systematic** observation of the
behavior, and (2) **Recording** the behavior with some
type of device (e.g., pencil and paper, golf counter).

This definition emphasizes the terms **systematic** and
recording. What we mean by systematic is that a

OBJECTIVES

By the end of this module, you will know:

- The definition of self-recording.
- The different ways in which behavior can be
  self-recorded.
- How to increase the effectiveness of self-
  recording as an intervention technique.
- How to implement a self-recording program.
- How to solve specific problems that may arise
  with a self-recording program.

specific behavior is defined and recorded over a predetermined period of time. For example, a behavior we want to record may be on-task classroom behavior, which is defined as "keeping one's eyes focused on either appropriate work materials or on a teacher who is giving instructions." The manner in which the behavior is recorded—either frequency, duration, or on latency—is important to define. **Frequency** involves counting the number of appropriate classroom student comments made. **Duration** includes how long a child works independently and appropriately. **Latency** might be the amount of time it takes a child to gather work materials and to get started working.

The amount of time over which the data are collected is important to specify. For example, a student might record during a single academic period or the whole day. If we do not know the amount of time involved, it would be difficult to determine what the data mean. For example, if a child self-recorded five talk-outs, does that mean five per hour, five per day, or five in the whole week? The time period is critical in making judgements and comparisons.

Some type of recording instrument is also needed for students to self-record. The most simple types of instruments generally include pencil and paper. Each time the behavior occurs, the child simply makes a mark on the paper. For duration and latency, some type of timing device is needed. A stopwatch, kitchen timer, or wristwatch can be used to record the length of a behavior. More exotic instruments include such devices as golf counters, pedometers (to collect data on movement), knitting counters (for counting), bracelets with beads that can be slid over a thread (like the beads on an abacus), or even videotapes of behavior. All self-recording involves some type of instrument to be used in collecting the data.

What Makes Self-Recording Effective?

Why self-record? Self-recording is important for two reasons. First, it offers **assessment** data on which to base decisions. However, what is more important is that self-recording actually **changes behavior**. If someone stares at us, we usually temporarily stop what we are doing and wonder about their attention. This phenomenon is called reactivity. In a sense, we react to the observer and change our behavior. This same reactive effect happens when we observe our own behavior, particularly if the behavior is an unconscious habit. When we collect data on ourselves, our unconscious pattern of behavior is interrupted and our behavior is temporarily changed. When we become accustomed to collecting these data, we frequently revert to old habits. A habit is temporarily broken when a smoker wraps his/her cigarettes in a piece of paper which is bound by a rubber band. Each time the person reaches for a cigarette, he/she has to unwrap the pack of cigarettes and write (self-record) on the paper that a cigarette was taken. This procedure will usually reduce smoking, at least temporarily, because the smoker will be surprised when he/she unconsciously reaches for the pack of cigarettes and finds it wrapped. This is what is meant by reactivity.

Reactivity actually changes the behavior that we are self-recording. It provides a window of opportunity to change a behavior that may be difficult to change through contingencies such as rewards and aversive consequences. If a student constantly daydreams, talks out, or impulsively disturbs other students, it may be difficult for him/her to change the behavior because it is such an ingrained habit. However, if the student self-records the inappropriate behavior, then the behavior may be decreased enough for the contingencies to work. For example, Jenson, Paoletti, and Petersen (1984) report a case in which a boy had a chronic throat clearing habit in class. In fact, the boy actually cleared his throat an average of 400 times per school day. This high rate of throat clearing was disturbing to the whole class.

When the researchers tried to apply a simple contingency of giving the boy points for reducing his throat clearing to 50 times per day or taking away points if occurrences went above 50, his throat clearing actually worsened and increased to approximately 450 times per day. Then the researchers removed the point contingency, gave the boy a golf counter, and asked him to record each time he cleared his throat. On the first day it fell below 50; thereafter, it slowly decreased. Then the researchers reimplemented the point contingency, and the throat clearing decreased to zero. In a sense, the self-recording, by temporarily reducing the throat clearings, gave the more permanent point contingency a chance to work.

When self-recording is used with unmotivated students, it is important to maximize the reactive effects of the procedure. The following variables have been shown to increase reactivity and the behavior change effects of self-recording (Haynes, 1978).

1. **Obtrusiveness**: The more obtrusive the recording method, then the more reactive are the self-recording procedures. Obtrusiveness means different to the point of standing out. For example, using a golf counter is more obtrusive than simply writing on a piece of paper. Or, recording on a blackboard is more obtrusive than recording on a small piece of paper taped on a desk.

2. **Behavior or Behavior-product**: It is actually better to self-record the actual occurrence of a behavior than the by-product of a behavior. For example, self-recording the number of problems actually completed is better than self-recording the grade on the math worksheet. Similarly, it is better to record the number of calories consumed at each meal than to record your weight in the morning.

3. **Prior or Following the Behavior**: In some instances, it may be better to self-record the behavior when it is just about to occur than to wait until it has occurred. For instance, it would be better to record each math problem just before it is attempted than to wait until after it is attempted. Again, with the eating example, you will lose more weight if you self-record just prior to taking a bite than if you wait until after you have taken a bite.

4. **Occurrence and Nonoccurrence**: It is better to record actual occurrences of a behavior than nonoccurrences. For example, Gottman and McFall (1972) studied class participation in a group of students in an alternative high school. They found that the largest increases in participation among the class happened when the students monitored the actual frequencies of their comments. A smaller increase was noted when the students monitored the frequency of times they actually wanted to make a comment but did not.

5. **Immediate Recording vs. Delayed Recording**: The closer the self-recording is to the actual behavior (i.e., either immediately before or immediately after), the more effective the procedure. For example, it is better when the child self-records immediately after making an inappropriate comment in the class, than waiting until the end of the period to mark the talk-outs. Some teachers think that having a child record during the middle of a lesson will be disruptive. However, research shows improvements in behaviors if self-recording occurs immediately.

> Contingencies make the temporary effects of self-recording more lasting.

6. **Positive and Negative Peer Social Contingencies**: Self-recording inappropriate behaviors generally results in a temporary reduction, and self-recording appropriate behaviors usually leads to a temporary increase. However, self-recording can backfire and make things worse in some situations. If a child is socially reinforced by his/her peers for inappropriate behavior, then self-recording those behaviors can actually cause them to increase. Similarly, if students are punished for appropriate behaviors by their peers, then these behaviors may actually decrease. Teachers should be aware of subtle peer reinforcement and, if it occurs, they should use a reinforcement contingency for the child or group.

7. **Contingencies**: The types of contingencies that teachers use are either positive rewards or mild aversives. Contingencies make the temporary effects of self-recording more lasting. As discussed previously, self-recording often gives the teacher a chance to get a foot in the door, and then to follow with a contingency. If contingencies (i.e., reinforcement and/or aversives) have failed when used alone, it is often wise to stop the contingency and then implement a self-recording procedure. When the self-recording produces positive results, then the contingency can be slowly resumed to make the effects more permanent.

Contingencies also work with self-recording if the results are opposite what the teacher wanted and if inappropriate peer social reinforcement is suspected (i.e., inappropriate behavior increases and/or appropriate behavior decreases). A contingency can be added for the whole group if the behavior reaches a predetermined desired level. For example, the group will receive ten minutes extra recess if Jeffery and Jamie's talk-outs are below three for the morning. Henderson (1986) used self-recording with a group contingency to increase both on-task behavior and academic productivity. With this procedure, a random "beep" was played by a cassette tape recorder in the classroom. Each row of students in the classroom formed a group, and one student recorded the on-task behavior of the whole row. When the beep sounded, if a child was off-task on the row, none of the children on that row would receive points, and no points were marked on the point card for that row. If all the children were on-task when the beep sounded, the child marked the point card. At the end of the period, all the students in the row received that number of points.

Enhancing the Effectiveness of a Self-Recording Program

Wanting To Improve

There is an old joke which says, "How many psychologists does it take to change a person's behavior? Only one, but the person has to really want to change." This is also true for self-recording. The procedure is much more effective for students who want to change, but who have difficulty because of bad habits or poor motivation. If a child expresses an interest in changing, self-recording can be very successful. However, it will also work on children who are less interested in changing, particularly if a positive motivation contingency is also used.

Goal Setting

The effects of self-recording can be enhanced if a predetermined goal is posted for the child. For example, a goal of 15 correct arithmetic problems for each child in a class can be posted on the blackboard. The children then self-record each problem they attempt during their arithmetic time. Simply having the goal posted and having each child check their problems off as they are done will generally help to increase the productivity of the group.

Problems Completed

Goal = 15 Problems

1 2 3 4 5 6 7 8 9 10 11 12 13 14 15 Finished

Self-Matching

The self-matching procedure is one of the most effective self-recording procedures for changing difficult classroom behaviors. With self-matching, a child records data on his/her own behavior. However, the teacher also randomly keeps track of one or two children in class, who are unaware that they are being monitored by the teacher. At the end of the day, the teacher announces which children were being monitored. The children are then asked to compare their ratings with the teacher's ratings. If there is a perfect match between the child and teacher, the child receives a reward (such as reinforcement points) plus a bonus; if there is a 90% match, the child just receives the points; if the match

is less than 90%, the child loses points. This procedure was used in a study by Rhode, Morgan, and Young (1983) to improve the behavior of behaviorally disordered children in a resource room and then in the regular classroom. The children's behavior and work was monitored for four periods each day and then matched with the teacher's ratings. The improvements in behavior and academics were dramatic. The basic advantage of self-matching is that it sensitizes a child to the teacher's perception and evaluation of his/her behavior.

Does Self-Recording Improve Academics?

To this point, we have mainly discussed the use of self-recording in changing classroom or social behavior. However, it can also be a powerful tool in changing basic academic skills. Several studies used self-recording with elementary through high school students to improve academic skills such as handwriting, completion of assignments, neatness of papers, arithmetic problems completed, history lessons, reading responses, and others (Andersen-Inman, Paine, & Deutchman, 1984; Holman & Baer, 1979; Knapczyk & Livingston, 1973; Piersel, 1985; Broden, Hall, & Mitts, 1971).

A particularly interesting application of self-recording was with an eighth grade girl, Liz, who expressed an interest in improving her grade in history (Broden et al., 1971). She was doing poorly in history ("D" grade), and approached the school counselor for help. The counselor scheduled weekly meetings to talk over her problem, but talking had little effect on behavior in the classroom. Liz continued to fail, was off-task frequently, and did not listen to the teacher's history lesson or instructions. The counselor then set up a self-recording program for Liz using the card form shown at the end of this module. She was told to record a "+" in a square when she had been studying and a "-" when she was not studying. No set time interval for recording was used in the history class. Liz was simply told to record her study behavior "when she thought of it."

The self-recording procedure improved Liz's classroom study time from 30% to approximately 80%. It is also interesting to note that when Liz increased her study behavior using the self-recording card, the history teacher spontaneously started to pay more positive attention to her. This is a natural positive contingency, which helped make Liz's change a permanent one. In fact, Liz passed this history course with a "C."

Does Self-Recording Change Behaviors That Interfere With Academics?

Again the answer is yes. Self-recording has been used to reduce several classroom disruptive behaviors that interfere with academic success. For example, self-recording has been used with classroom talk-outs, off-task, and out-of-seat behavior (Broden et al., 1971; Sugai & Rowe, 1984; Rooney, Hallahan, & Lloyd, 1984; McLaughlin; 1984). In the same paper as the study with Liz, Broden et al. (1971) tried self- recording with another child who had a talk-out problem. Stu ("the motor mouth") was an eighth grade boy who had a high rate of inappropriately talking out and disturbing others in his math class. Stu's talk-out rate was split into two different time periods, A and B. In section A, his talk-out rate was 1.1 per minute and in section B it was 1.6 per minute. This is an extremely high rate. A slip of paper like the one pictured here was given to Stu and he was told to record his talk-outs in the math class. Talk-outs dropped to .3 per minute in section A and .5 per minute in section B. When Stu was not given the slips on which to self-record, the behavior immediately worsened.

> Self-recording has been used to reduce several classroom disruptive behaviors that interfere with academic success.

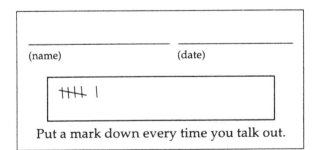

(name) _____ (date) _____

████

| ~~HHH~~ |

Put a mark down every time you talk out.

It is of note that Stu was not particularly interested in using the self-recording procedure. Even though he was not motivated, the procedure had a substantial positive impact on his behavior. To make the change permanent, a teacher should implement a program of praise for his reduction in talk-outs and possibly some type of reward contingency.

How to Set Up a Self-Recording Program In a Classroom

There are several questions that a teacher should answer before using a self-recording program. First, is the program needed or can the child simply change behavior if asked? Second, does the behavior seem like a habit, or is it impulsive? If a habit, then the procedure will probably work. Third, what kind of recording instrument is needed? A pencil and paper system is probably best for most classrooms. Fourth, is there peer encouragement for misbehavior? If so, a contingency may be needed for the whole classroom.

There are just a few materials a teacher needs in order to implement a self-recording procedure. A teacher will need a recording device such as a pencil and paper, golf counter, or knitting counter. Some type of simple form is also needed that defines the target behavior and includes space to record the data. Forms are shown at the end of this module that can be copied and used. A teacher trying to improve on-task behavior might also need some type of random signalling device. This device can be a kitchen timer, or a cassette player with a tape that contains random beeps or numbers.

STEP ONE

Talk about the procedure with the child and solicit his/her help. This may enhance the motivation of the child, which will make the self-recording procedure work better.

STEP TWO

Specifically define the behavior so you and the child understand what you want. For example, "Talk-outs are saying something in class without the teacher's permission." Or, "Correct math problems, are attempted math problems that are checked by the teacher."

STEP THREE

Discuss the recording instrument. If it is a pencil and paper method, then it is best for the teacher to supply these.

STEP FOUR

Define the time over which you want the recordings to occur (e.g., an academic period or the whole day).

STEP FIVE

Decide if there appears to be peer support for inappropriate behavior. Do other children encourage the child to talk out or be off-task? If they do, then implement a group contingency for the whole class or the most troublesome children.

STEP SIX

Check on the validity of the child's self-recording. For example, the number of correct math problems could be checked or a teacher can also keep his/her own tally of the inappropriate talk-outs made by the child. If a child is obviously in error or is cheating, then the teacher can prompt the child when the behavior next occurs. Or, the teacher can implement a self-matching program.

STEP SEVEN

Have some type of graph or data collection system that you can use to decide if the child is improving. A simple graph with days on the bottom and the target behavior on the left side is all that is needed.

STEP EIGHT

Decide if some type of additional reward and/or mild aversive contingency is needed to produce a permanent change in the behavior. Remember, the contingency does not have to be elaborate. Something as simple as increased teacher praise for the appropriate behavior or reviewing the progress with the child is sometimes all that is needed. In more difficult cases, a simple contract or periodic reward can be used (e.g., if you improve your study time by keeping your off-tasks to below five in the reading period, then you can have five minutes of free time).

Cautions

There are a few cautions related to self-recording. First, teachers should be sensitive to the reactions of other children in the classroom. For example, the self-recording child should not stand out or be the butt of student comments. It is also important to make sure that the child can actually perform the required target behavior that is being self-recorded. If the child cannot perform the behavior, he/she may get frustrated and may act-out. The ability to use the self-recording procedure is also important. The child must be capable of using a pencil or of understanding what is expected and how it should be rated or self-recorded.

Troubleshooting a Self-Recording Program

PROBLEM: *The self-recording program was working, but later appeared to lose its effectiveness.*

> **Solution:** This is a common problem. It generally means that the child has become accustomed to the self-recording program and, therefore, it is no longer reactive. There are two possible solutions. First, change the self-recording instrument and make the new instrument more obtrusive. For example, if the child was using a pencil and paper to self-record, change it to a golf counter or some other instrument. Second, try a reward contingency if the child stops responding. Remember, the effects of self-recording are temporary unless they are consistently rewarded or praised. The best solution may a combination of both suggestions.

PROBLEM: *The inappropriate behavior is increasing rather than decreasing.*

> **Solution:** The first thing to check is peer reinforcement for the misbehavior (e.g., smiles, snickers, looks of congratulation, looks of approval, notes being passed after misbehavior, gestures such as thumbs-up). In a sense, self-recording is actually making the child more skilled at misbehaving so that he/she can be reinforced by his/her peers. The solution is to continue the self-recording but make improvements in the child's appropriate behavior a group contingency (i.e., the whole group earns a reward or loses something dependent on the self-recorded behavior).

PROBLEM: *The inappropriate behavior is increasing rather than decreasing, and there is no evidence of peer reinforcement for the misbehavior.*

Solution: In this case, the child probably did not want to change his/her behavior, and self-recording has made things worse. In addition, the behavior that is being self-recorded is probably important to the child in obtaining some type of reinforcement from the environment. The best thing to do is to continue the self-recording, but put a contingency into effect so that if the child improves, a small reinforcer can be earned. It is also important to have the teacher increase his/her praise for appropriate behavior. Frequently, the inappropriate behavior that is being self-recorded served the purpose of getting the teacher's negative attention. Even though the attention would appear negative to most people, it probably served as a reinforcer for the child's inappropriate behavior.

PROBLEM: *The target behavior has stayed the same but other misbehaviors have increased.*

Solution: This an interesting situation. If this occurs, then there is a good chance that the child is incapable of performing the target behavior. This is often true with academic behaviors or behaviors that require performance in front of a group (e.g., math problems, writing assignments, making appropriate verbal comments about a classroom topic, or speaking in front of class). The increase in other inappropriate behaviors is probably the result of frustration at not being able to perform the required target behavior. The only thing to do in this situation is to give the child additional instruction in the required academic task with generous praise and little punishment. For performance problems, such as speaking in front of class or making appropriate verbal comments, it is best to have the child practice the response with the teacher in a safe situation (i.e., alone with the teacher). Videotapes of the child performing the correct response can often help. It may also require a "student confederate" to praise the child when he/she makes a comment or presentation (e.g., "Good remark," "I wish I had thought of that," "Nice going.").

PROBLEM: *The child wants to self-record, but either does not have the ability to keep track of the target behaviors, or does not seem to understand the recording procedure.*

Solution: The key to this is to simplify the target behaviors and the recording procedures. **Countoons** can help. These are cartoons of the actual behaviors that you want the child to self-record. Countoons can be designed for: (1) Independent seat work, (2) Getting work done on time, and (3) Raising hand to make a comment. All of these countoons would be rated on a simple 1 to 3 scale (i.e., 1 = poor, 2 = OK, 3= good).

References

Andersen-Inman, L., Paine, S.C., & Deutchman, L. (1984). Neatness counts: Effects of direct instruction and self-monitoring on the transfer of neat-paper skills to nontraining settings. *Analysis and Intervention in Developmental Disabilities, 4*(2),137-155.

Broden, M., Hall, R., & Mitts, B. (1971). The effect of self-recording on the classroom behavior of two eighth grade students. *Journal of Applied Behavior Analysis, 4*(3), 191-199.

Gottman, J.M. & McFall, R.M. (1972). Self-monitoring effects in a program for potential high school dropouts: A time series analysis. *Journal of Consulting and Clinical Psychology, 39*(2), 273-281.

Haynes, S.N. (1978). *Principles of behavioral assessment.* New York: Gardner.

Henderson, H.S. (1986). Using variable interval schedules to improve on-task behavior in the classroom. *Education and Treatment of Children, 9*(3), 250-263.

Holman, J. & Baer, D.M. (1979). Facilitating generalization of on-task behavior through self-monitoring of academic tasks. *Journal of Autism and Developmental Disorders, 9*(4), 429-446.

Jenson, W.R., Paoletti, P., & Petersen, B.P. (1984). Self-monitoring plus a reinforcement contingency to reduce a chronic throat clearing tic in a child. *Behavior Therapist, 7*(10), 192.

Knapczyk, D.R. & Livingston, C. (1973). Self-recording and student teacher supervision: Variables within a token economy structure. *Journal of Applied Behavior Analysis, 6*(3),481-486.

McLaughlin, T.F. (1984). A comparison of self-recording and self-recording plus consequences for on-task and assignment completion. *Contemporary Educational Psychology, 9*(2), 185-192.

Piersel, W.C. (1985). Self-observation and completion of school assignments: The influence of a physical recording device and expectancy characteristics. *Psychology in the Schools, 22*(3), 331-336.

Rhode, G., Morgan, D.P., & Young, R.K. (1983). Generalization and maintenance of treatment gains of behaviorally handicapped students from classrooms using self-evaluation procedures. *Journal of Applied Behavior Analysis, 16*(2), 171-188.

Rooney, K., Hallahan, D., & Lloyd, J.W. (1984). Self-recording of attention by learning disabled students in the regular classroom. *Journal of Learning Disabilities, 17*(6), 360-364.

Sugai, G. & Rowe, P. (1984). The effect of self-recording on out-of-seat behavior of an EMR student. *Education and Training of the Mentally Retarded, 19*(1), 23-28.

Self-Recording Form—
Study Habits

_____
(NAME)   (DATE)

At the top of the page are several rows of squares. At different times during the class period, put down a "+" if you are studying, a "−" if you aren't. Mark a square whenever you think of it, but do not mark all the squares at the same time.

Self-Recording Form—
Study Habits

_____
(NAME)   (DATE)

At the top of the page are several rows of squares. At different times during the class period, put down a "+" if you are studying, a "−" if you aren't. Mark a square whenever you think of it, but do not mark all the squares at the same time.

Self-Recording Form—
Study Habits

_____
(NAME)   (DATE)

At the top of the page are several rows of squares. At different times during the class period, put down a "+" if you are studying, a "−" if you aren't. Mark a square whenever you think of it, but do not mark all the squares at the same time.

Self-Recording Form—
Study Habits

_____
(NAME)   (DATE)

At the top of the page are several rows of squares. At different times during the class period, put down a "+" if you are studying, a "−" if you aren't. Mark a square whenever you think of it, but do not mark all the squares at the same time.

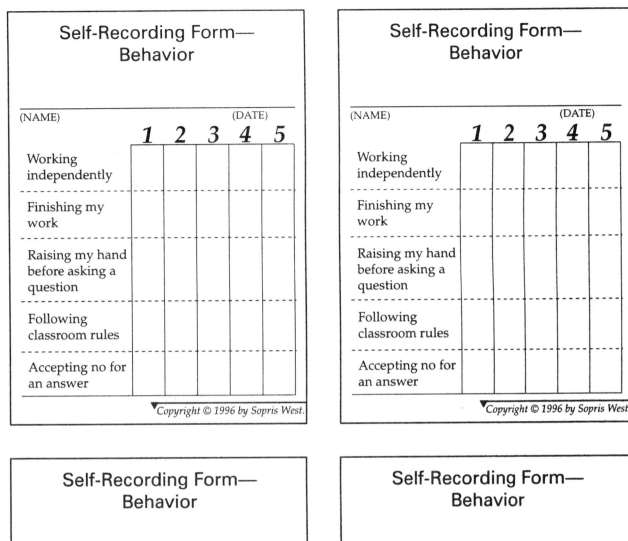

Self-Recording Form— Behavior

(NAME)   (DATE)

	1	2	3	4	5
Working independently					
Finishing my work					
Raising my hand before asking a question					
Following classroom rules					
Accepting no for an answer					

Copyright © 1996 by Sopris West.

Self-Recording Form— Behavior

(NAME)   (DATE)

	1	2	3	4	5
Working independently					
Finishing my work					
Raising my hand before asking a question					
Following classroom rules					
Accepting no for an answer					

Copyright © 1996 by Sopris West.

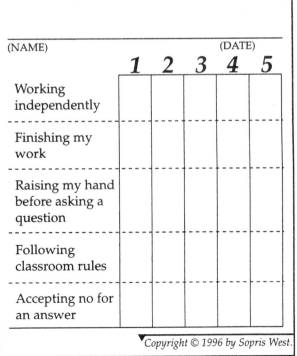

Self-Recording Form— Behavior

(NAME)   (DATE)

	1	2	3	4	5
Working independently					
Finishing my work					
Raising my hand before asking a question					
Following classroom rules					
Accepting no for an answer					

Copyright © 1996 by Sopris West.

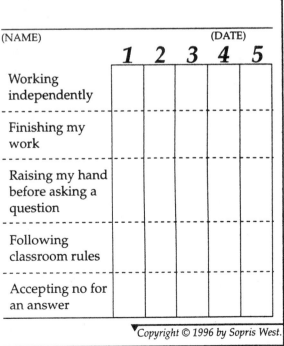

Self-Recording Form— Behavior

(NAME)   (DATE)

	1	2	3	4	5
Working independently					
Finishing my work					
Raising my hand before asking a question					
Following classroom rules					
Accepting no for an answer					

Copyright © 1996 by Sopris West.

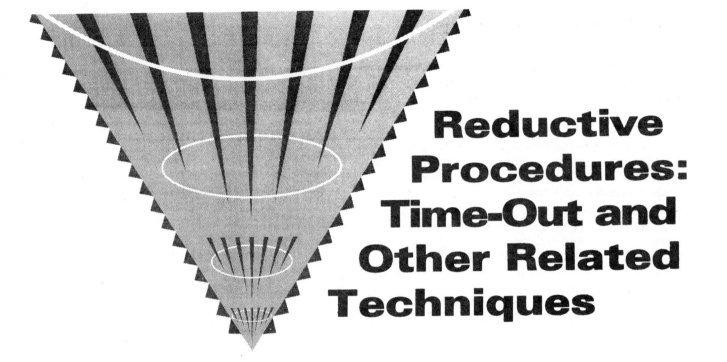

Reductive Procedures: Time-Out and Other Related Techniques

by William R. Jenson, Ph.D., University of Utah, and H. Kenton Reavis, Ed.D., Utah State Office of Education

What is Time-Out?

There are several misconceptions about time-out. Some believe that time-out is placing a child in a secluded room, making the child sit in a corner, or even sending a child to in-school suspension. Time-out is more than these limited examples. Time-out can be defined as: removing a child from a reinforcing environment and placing him/her in a nonreinforcing environment, as an aversive consequence of a specific misbehavior.

It can be seen from this definition that time-out is not limited to a specific place or location. Instead, the main idea is that time-out must be less reinforcing than the situation in which the misbehavior occurs.

If a classroom in which a misbehavior occurs is stale and nonreinforcing, and a teacher places a child in

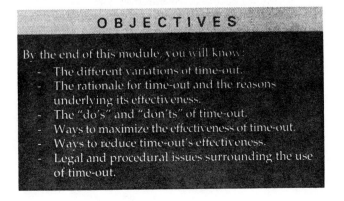

OBJECTIVES

By the end of this module, you will know:

- The different variations of time-out.
- The rationale for time-out and the reasons underlying its effectiveness.
- The "do's" and "don'ts" of time-out.
- Ways to maximize the effectiveness of time-out.
- Ways to reduce time-out's effectiveness.
- Legal and procedural issues surrounding the use of time-out.

the school office (which may be more lively than the classroom), then the teacher is actually reinforcing the child. The school office, in this example, is not time-out; rather, it is a positively reinforcing environment.

The Time-Out Continuum

The nonreinforcing environments that are used in time-out can be conceptualized on a continuum. The least restrictive part of this continuum leaves a student in the classroom at his/her desk, or at least still in the instructional setting. An intermediate form of time-out may remove the student from the desk and place him/her in a corner of the classroom. The most restrictive form of time-out involves removing the student from the classroom and placing him/her in a separate room. Teachers should always begin with the least restrictive time-out unless a student's behavior is dangerous to self, others, or property, or if the Individualized Education Plan (IEP) recommends otherwise. If less restrictive forms of time-out are not effective, then a teacher should proceed along the continuum until an effective procedure is found.

> . . . withdrawal of materials is an easy time-out procedure that is often overlooked.

Types of Time-Out

Some of these procedures are straightforward, while others are more complex and require more planning.

1. **Planned Ignoring**: This is the simplest form of time-out. Planned ignoring involves the systematic removal of social reinforcement (attention) by the teacher for a specific amount of time. When the student misbehaves, the teacher breaks eye contact, turns away, and stops all social interaction with the student. In essence, the student is placed in a less reinforcing environment because the teacher does not interact with him/her. Planned ignoring assumes that the teacher's social attention is reinforcing. If it is not, then this procedure will not work. The teacher should also be prepared for an extinction burst in the early stages of the procedure. In an extinction burst, the student tries harder (by misbehaving) to get the teacher's attention. If the teacher falters and attends (even with negative attention) to the student during a burst of misbehavior, then the student is reinforced

and will be more resistive to this technique in the future.

2. **Withdrawal of Materials**: This is the next step in the time-out gradient. With the withdrawal of materials, a student's academic or work materials are withdrawn without comment and the student simply sits at his/her desk. The teacher and the rest of the class ignore the student until the materials are returned at the end of the time-out period. This form of time-out is effective if the student is relatively compliant and will sit without disturbing other students. It does not work if the student is disruptive. However, withdrawal of materials is an easy time-out procedure that is often overlooked.

3. **Timing-Out an Object (Bumpy Bunny)**: This technique is more of a response cost procedure than a time-out procedure, but it works well with younger students. In timing-out an object, a favored object or toy (e.g., a stuffed toy such as a bunny) that a student is allowed to have in the classroom is taken away when the student misbehaves and timed-out for a specified period of time. The object can be placed on the teacher's desk or in a special time-out drawer. The technique works well when a student is normally allowed to have the object on his/her person or desk, and when this is viewed as a special privilege. Small toys, pictures of family, hats, a special pencil sharpener, or something to play with at recess or free time work well as the objects. For older students, a Walkman® or Game Boy® would be very suitable. A problem with this procedure occurs if the student plays with the object during class time. The contingency should be an automatic object time-out for playing with the object without permission. An additional problem can occur if a student resists giving the object to the teacher. In general, however, this is a useful technique that may be underused.

4. **Time-Out Ribbon**: The time-out ribbon technique is a procedure that was developed by Foxx and Shapiro (1978). To implement this technique, a teacher needs to make a simple ribbon that a student wears around his/her neck. While a student is wearing the ribbon, he/she participates in normal classroom activities. However, when the student misbehaves, the ribbon is removed for a period of time and the student is ignored by the teacher and the class. This procedure allows the student to stay

at his/her desk. The ribbon works very well with younger students and students with developmental delays. Most students feel that the ribbon is special, and they like it. The author has used the time-out ribbon procedure with several students when other time-out procedures have failed for particularly difficult behaviors such as classroom masturbation and inappropriate laughter. The time-out ribbon shares the same problems as other time-out procedures. In addition, the procedure is inappropriate if the student resists the teacher's removal of the ribbon.

5. **Contingent Observation Time-Out**: With contingent observation, the student is removed from his/her desk for misbehaving and is usually placed in a chair away from the main classroom activities for a short period of time. The student is allowed to observe the classroom and its activities, but not allowed to participate. While in the chair, the student is ignored by the teacher and other students. In theory, this time-out procedure is effective because the student is not allowed to interact, but instead observes what he/she is missing. Contingent observation works well with compliant students with minor problems who will sit in a chair. It does not work well with students who repeatedly get out of the chair or try to interact with other students.

6. **No-Look Time-Out**: This technique is essentially the same as contingent observation, except that the student is not allowed to observe the classroom activities. Usually, the student is placed in a part of the classroom that does not allow viewing of the classroom activities. For example, the student might be placed in the corner of the classroom. Or, a chair might be turned to the wall or a student might be placed behind a screen. This is a more restrictive form of time-out, and is useful when planned ignoring or contingent observation has not worked. Problems occur with no-look time-out if the student will not stay in the chair, throws objects over a screen, or makes disturbing noises. It is important that no-look time-out does not include placing a student in a separate room that might be contained within a classroom (e.g., a closet, bathroom, or empty room). Placing a student in these kinds of areas is one of the most restrictive forms of time-out.

7. **Head Down Time-Out**: A simpler form of a visual screening (see item number 12) time-out procedure, which has been used by teachers for a long time, is a simple head down on the desk procedure. For time-out, a student is told to close his/her eyes and put his/her head on the desk for a specified period of time. This procedure is like a visual screen in that the student cannot see what is going on in the classroom; however, it does not require a cloth screen. Head on the desk works for relatively compliant students, but is ineffective if a student refuses. Students should never be physically forced to put their head down.

8. **Time-Out to the Hall**: This is a common form of time-out that teachers frequently employ, using a desk or chair that is placed in the hall. Hall time-out is used when the student is too disruptive for a less restrictive form of time-out. A major problem with hall time-out is that the student is left unsupervised in a hall where adults and other students pass by and may talk to or pay attention to the student. In addition, the student may have access to all types of potential sources of reinforcement (e.g., drinking fountains, other students' lockers, coats on a rack, and running in the hall). Overall, hall time-out is an ineffective form of time-out and generally should not be used.

9. **Time-Out to Another Classroom**: Time-out to another classroom can be an effective form of time-out. However, the teacher should follow a set of preplanned steps: (1) Arrange with another teacher to use his/her classroom; (2) Pick a different grade level classroom (generally, a two-year difference in grade level is best); (3) Decide on the length of time for the contingency (e.g., 30 minutes); (4) Have a desk or table set up at which the student can work; (5) Have academic work materials available for the student, and (6) Offer to reciprocate by allowing the other teacher to send time-out students to your classroom.

10. **In-School Suspension (ISS)**: This procedure is a form of extended time-out wherein a student is suspended from the classroom **for long periods of time** (e.g., one day) and required to work in another school setting. Generally, the in-school suspension environment can be a separate classroom set aside just for this purpose. It is essential that students be supervised for the entire time they spend in in-school suspension. Also, students should be required to do academic work in this environment. (NOTE: For more detail on this technique, refer to the module on in-school suspension.)

11. **Time-Out to a Room**: Time-out to a room involves placing a student in a separate room that is designated as the "time-out room." It is critical that this room be clean, well-lighted, not frightening, and not a danger to a student. In addition, the time-out room should not be used for any other purpose (e.g., storage, mail, printing) than time-out. A person should always be outside the room, and a window or peep hole (i.e., 180 degree apartment house peep hole) should be installed so the student can be observed. It is also best to design the room so that the adult on the outside must hold the door handle in a locked position. When the door handle is released by the adult, it automatically springs back into an unlocked position and the student can simply push the door from the inside and get out. It is best that there be either no door handle inside the room, or that the door handle on the student's side does not turn. This will avoid a struggle between the adult and the student. Having an adult hold the door handle in the locked position ensures that there will always be a person outside the door when a student is in the room (the student is never left unattended).

12. **Visual Screening Time-Out**: The visual screening time-out technique is a rarely used procedure. It is sometimes used with students with mental retardation or autism who use their eyes when self-stimulating. The student wears a cloth headband and, when he/she engages in misbehavior such as self-stimulating with the hands or inappropriate bizarre laughter, the band is placed around his/her eyes for a short period of time. The student remains at his/her desk in the classroom. If they try to take the band from their eyes, they are gently manually guided to put their hands down. If other types of time-out have failed, this procedure works well with students who would self-stimulate with their eyes. It is not a procedure that would be used with students with minor behavior problems; it should be reserved for students with more severe disorders.

The major drawback with this procedure is that someone (aide, volunteer, parent, or teacher) must stay with the student when the procedure is used in case the student tries to remove the band. It is also important that the headband be made of soft material with elastic in the back. The band should never totally cover the student's head or obstruct breathing by covering the nose.

13. **Movement Suppression Time-out**: This time-out procedure is probably the most restrictive form of time-out and should be used for only the most severe types of behavior (e.g., self-injury or aggression). In movement suppression, a student is required to stand against a wall, touching the wall with his/her chin, both hands behind the back with one hand on top of the other, and the toes of both feet touching the wall. An adult stands behind the student and firmly reprimands if movement or talk occurs (e.g., "Don't move" or "Don't talk"). Generally, this procedure lasts about three minutes. Teachers are cautioned that specific training is essential for correct implementation. This procedure should not be used without team/administrative involvement.

Pre-Implementation Procedures

Time-out has great potential for misuse and abuse if staff are untrained, or if implementation is inconsistent. To ensure that procedures are followed, it is best to:

1. Require each staff member to read the procedures and take a test on the content. Keep the test results on file and periodically review them with each staff member.

2. Keep each staff member's tests on file to document their basic knowledge of the procedure. This helps answer the question, "Were your staff trained in using the procedure before they tried it on a student?"

3. Have each staff member experience the time-out procedure (i.e., role play the procedure and have them spend a time-out period in the time-out environment). Having the staff experience the procedure can be used to answer questions such as, "Have you ever tried the procedure?" or "Did you try the procedure on yourself before you tried it on a student?"

> Time-out has great potential for misuse and abuse if staff are untrained, or if implementation is inconsistent.

4. Always have the time-out procedures on file and have the procedures taped to the time-out room door. If the procedures are also on

the time-out room door, it is difficult for staff members to say they have never seen them or they have forgotten the procedures.

Procedures for Implementing Time-Out

The general procedures for implementing time-out are as follows:

The time-out room should only be implemented after it has been discussed and agreed to by the student's parent(s). The procedure should be described on the student's IEP with the inappropriate behaviors objectively defined.

The "What is Time-Out?" form should be signed by the parent(s) and a staff member.

The full procedure should be described to the student before the procedure is implemented. It is a good idea to show the student and the parents the time-out room if one is used.

A time-out room log (see sample at end of this module) should be maintained and used each time the time-out room procedure is used. This log should include: (1) Student's name, (2) Person responsible for the student while they are in time-out, (3) Date the procedure was used, (4) Time the student went in the room, (5) Time the student came out, (6) The behavior that resulted in time-out, and (7) A comments section for reporting unusual incidents.

The inappropriate behaviors for which the time-out room procedure is used should be very serious (e.g., aggression, property destruction, tantrums, severe noncompliance). The procedure should not be used for minor behaviors (e.g., crying, off-task, tardiness, classroom talk-outs).

The length of time for time-out generally works out to one minute per year of the age of the student (i.e., a six-year old student would have a six-minute time-out; a ten-year old would have a ten-minute time-out).

A timer (e.g., a 60-minute kitchen timer) should be set. When the timer rings, the student should be quiet for at least 30 seconds before he/she can be released. If the student is released during a tantrum or while screaming, these behaviors are reinforced.

As a rule, a student should not spend more than 55 consecutive minutes in the time-out room. The exact maximum length will vary in different states and school districts. The teacher should know what this policy is for his/her school district.

For all forms of time-out, when a student misbehaves, he/she should be told to go to time-out. After the student has been given this direction, the staff member should not talk with him/her (either while going to time-out or while the student is in time-out).

If the student refuses to go to the time-out room, the staff members can use manual guidance to escort the student to time-out if they are reasonably sure they can manage the student without a danger to themselves or the student. If there is such a danger, the staff member may need the help of additional staff. Specific training is required before manual guidance is employed.

If a student refuses to go to the time-out room, the staff may want to add one minute to the time-out period each time a staff member tells the student to go to time-out. For example, if a ten-year old boy refuses to go to time-out and argues, then the staff may say, "Now it is 11 minutes." If the student refuses to comply after your second request, enlist the assistance of additional staff to help place the student in time-out.

If the student defecates or urinates while in time-out, he/she should be required to clean up the mess under supervision.

If a student destroys part of the time-out room, then the parent(s) should be consulted. Possibly, a special toy or privilege can be kept until the student helps repair the damage (after school or on a weekend).

If the student refuses to come out of time-out after the procedure is over, then wait. A student can be left in the time-out room with the door open while the teacher or aide stands outside ignoring him or her. The worst thing to do is to plead with the student to come out of time-out. Simply wait: sooner or later he or she will exit.

Maximizing the Effectiveness of Time-Out

It is important to specify the behaviors (such as aggression, swearing, noncompliance, and tantruming) that lead to time-out, so the student can avoid them.

There are several techniques that can make time-out more effective in the classroom. Simple procedural adaptations can change an ineffective time-out procedure to an effective one. These techniques are as follows:

1. **Making the Classroom Reinforcing**: One of the common problems that makes time-out ineffective is an unpleasant classroom atmosphere. Boredom, lack of stimulation, and an emphasis on negative management techniques significantly reduce the reinforcing power of the classroom. Remember, the definition of time-out involves being placed in a nonreinforcing environment as a result of inappropriate behavior. If a classroom is unpleasant, the student may prefer to spend time in time-out rather than in the classroom. Make an effort to increase the reinforcing value of the classroom. For example, set a goal of a certain number of social reinforcers that you will give to the class. All of these reinforcers do not have to be directed to problem students. For example, make a rule that you will give the class at least 30 social reinforcers each day (that is five per hour over a six-hour day). The problem student should get at least five of these reinforcers. In addition, improve the reinforcing value of the classroom by: (1) Adding mystery motivators, (2) Implementing classroom games, (3) Adding some snacks, (4) Putting in a classroom spinner for good behavior, or (5) Varying the classroom schedule with a story or free time activity.

2. **Reinforcing the Student for Not Going to Time-Out**: It sometimes helps to develop a contract with a student wherein he/she is reinforced for not going to time-out. In a sense, you are reinforcing behaviors that are incompatible with those that lead to time-out. It is important to specify the behaviors (such as aggression, swearing, noncompliance, and tantruming) that lead to time-out, so the student can avoid them. A contract might stipulate that a student will get 15 minutes free time plus the chance at a mystery motivator if he avoids time-out for the day.

3. **Explaining Time-Out to the Student**: It generally helps to explain the time-out procedure before it is begun. The explanation should include a description of the behaviors that lead to time-out, what types of time-out will be used, and what will happen if the student resists the time-out procedure. The explanation should be provided when things are calm in the classroom. The teacher should not argue with the student about the procedures or negotiate the procedures. They should be handled in a matter-of-fact way.

4. **Combining the Time-Out Procedure With Warnings and Rule Statement Procedures**: It helps to use a warning procedure that time-out will be used if a request is not complied with. For example, a teacher might use the word "need" in a request to signal that time-out will follow in a short time if the request is not followed. For instance, the teacher might say, "Jeffrey, you need to stop arguing with me." If Jeffrey does not stop, then time-out could be used.

Teachers can also re-state the rule before using time-out. For example, the teacher might state, "The classroom rule is no hitting," and then the student would be placed in time-out. Rule stating is different from a warning procedure because with rule stating, the student has already broken a classroom rule. However, rule stating helps because it underscores which behaviors lead to time-out. It is important not to argue about whether a rule was broken, or about extenuating circumstances. Simply state the classroom rule and then proceed with the time-out procedure.

5. **Having to Sit and Watch**: It helps with some students if they have to sit and watch for a brief period of time after a time-out (to another classroom, in-school suspension, or to a time-out room). For example, a student who has returned from a time-out room would have to sit in a chair for two minutes and watch the classroom activities before being allowed to go to his/her desk. Watching appears to settle some students down after a time-out period.

6. **Varying the Time-Out Period**: Some students want to control any situation, including the time they spend in time-out. These students often tell a teacher that the time-out period is over and they should be released. If a time-out procedure was initially effective but has lost its potency, and if the student is very controlling, then varying the actual time period is a good

procedure. It helps not to tell the student the exact time you are using. For example, if the student is eight years old and you have been using an eight-minute period of time, it might be more effective to randomly vary the time around an eight minute average. For instance, one period might be six minutes, one period eight minutes, and another period ten minutes. You should secure permission from the student's parent(s) to use this variation.

7. **Varying Time-Out With Other Procedures**: It can also be useful to randomly vary the time-out procedure with other mildly aversive procedures. This is particularly effective for students who appear to have adapted to the time-out technique. To randomly vary a procedure, the teacher would pick three procedures such as time-out, overcorrection, and response cost. When a student misbehaves, the teacher randomly implements one of the three procedures. It is important to preselect the techniques to be used. Of course, this procedure will be far less effective if the student is told which technique will be used next.

8. **Combining Time-Out With a Group Contingency**: If a student is socially reinforced by his/her peers for misbehaving, it becomes very difficult to change the misbehavior. Many students with behavioral disorders are especially reinforced by the effects of their misbehavior on peers (e.g., smiling, snickering, clapping, or being congratulated for going to time-out). A simple test to see if a student is reinforced by peers is to watch the student just after he/she misbehaves. If the student looks around at peers or solicits support, he/she is being socially reinforced. To counter such pressure, a group contingency can be used. The whole group can lose a privilege if a problem student goes to time-out or can earn an extra privilege if he/she does not go to time-out.

9. **Using a Tape Recorder with Time-Out**: Students sometimes misbehave in public places where there are no time-out facilities, such as on a field trip or while riding a school bus. In such cases, a teacher can record the misbehavior on a small tape recorder. This procedure works best if the student verbally argues or loudly tantrums. When the students and teacher return to school where there are time-out facilities, the tape is played back to the student, who is then sent to time-out. This procedure might also be used with video recording. A video camera would be particularly useful for nonverbal misbehavior that an audio recorder would miss.

10. **Re-creating the Scene**: This technique can also be used for misbehaviors that have already occurred and where a time delay before time-out can be used. Essentially, with re-creating the scene, a student is required to re-create the misbehavior under the supervision of an adult and then is consequated with a time-out procedure. For example, Van Houten and Rolider (1988) used this technique with an autistic student, Shawn, who bit other students. The victim was seated on the floor in the same place he had been when he was bitten and instructed to simulate crying when Shawn's face came close to the victim's cheek. Next, the experimenter firmly grasped Shawn's head with a palm on each cheek to ensure complete control and thereby preclude the possibility of Shawn's biting the student again. Shawn's head was guided toward the student's cheek and his teeth exposed by gently pulling back his lips. As Shawn's teeth came within several inches of the victim's face, Shawn received a loud reprimand in the form of "Don't bite" while the experimenter placed a pointed finger in front of his face. Shawn was then quickly taken to the nearest corner in the play area, and a one-minute movement suppression time-out procedure was applied. This procedure was then repeated two more times.

The re-creating the scene procedure is very restrictive and should be used with only the most serious behaviors. However, it is extremely effective for behaviors that are not directly observed. In addition to biting, it has been used with tantrums and with stealing. Again, a teacher should use this procedure only after the student's parent(s) and the victim's parent(s) give their consent.

Procedures to Avoid When Implementing Time-Out

Just as there is a set of procedures to improve the effectiveness of time-out, there are also procedures that reduce the effectiveness of time-out. They are:

1. **Over-Explaining Time-Out**: It is important to explain time-out procedures to students and orient them to the time-out facilities. However, once is enough. Many teachers think they must

continually explain time-out; sometimes they argue with students about time-out procedures. Sometimes teachers use explanation after explanation because they are reluctant to use time-out, thinking that if they explain the procedures to their students again, then they may not need to use time-out. Similarly, teachers frequently will over-explain and threaten. For example, a teacher might say "Do you understand that if you continue to misbehave, I'm going to use time-out with you?"

Repeated explanations combined with threats reduce the effectiveness of time-out. Explain it once thoroughly, and then implement the procedure. If you feel the student still does not understand, wait until you are in a neutral situation and then explain the procedure again.

2. **Talking During the Time-Out Procedure**: This problem occurs in two ways. First, the teacher talks with the student while they are going to time-out. It is important to keep the conversation to a minimum while going to time-out. Explaining to students what they did wrong, emotional reprimands, or just plain feeling guilty should not be reasons to start a conversation while implementing the time-out procedure. Second, once the student is in time-out, the teacher should not respond to him/her. This does not mean that the teacher should not supervise or observe the student. However, neither does it mean that the teacher should talk to the student in time-out. Common mistakes involving talking with a student in time-out include such instances as:

   - Answering questions concerning how much more time they will be in time-out.
   - Arguing about the misbehaviors or about the fairness of being placed in time-out.
   - Responding to threats about what the student is going to do when he/she gets out of time-out.
   - Trying to calm the student down or to urge him/her to stop tantruming.

Once a student is in time-out, he/she should be ignored and communication kept to zero (even if he/she swears at you), unless there is an emergency.

3. **Slowly Increasing the Time Period Used with Time-Out (The Swimming Pool Effect)**: There is a real temptation to start with very short periods of time for time-out and to slowly increase them. For example, a teacher may use only 30 seconds of time-out for a seven-year old student. At first, 30 seconds may be effective, but it will slowly lose its effectiveness because it is too short. Then the teacher may increase 30 seconds to one minute, then two minutes, then five minutes, and so on up to excessively long periods of time (over 30 minutes). When this happens, it is the same as jumping into a cold swimming pool. First you put a toe in, then another toe, then a foot, then a leg, until the whole body is submerged and you are adapted to the cool water. Likewise, we adapt the student to long periods of time-out. This is a trap. The teacher should use the most effective time period that will make time-out work. This is generally one minute for each year of age. A seven-year old student would need seven minutes of time-out.

4. **Letting the Students Determine Their Own Time-Out Period**: Some teachers think a student should determine the length of time-out. A teacher might say, "Go to time-out and come out when you can behave". This is a mistake, particularly with very difficult students. They will go to time-out, spend a very short period of time, and then return and misbehave again. Self-determined time-out periods do not work. Teachers must determine the length of time, and it should not be negotiable. Again, one minute per year is a good guideline for most students.

5. **Not Using a Quiet Time at the End of Time-Out**: At the end of the designated time-out period, the student should be quiet for a short period of time (e.g., 30 seconds). If the student is let out of time-out during a tantrum, when he/she is screaming or threatening, then he/she is reinforced for these behaviors. For example, at the end of seven minutes for a seven-year old, if the student is screaming and beating on the door, then the teacher should wait until the student is quiet. It is a mistake to say to the student, "If you are quiet, then time-out will end," because to give any attention to a student in time-out is reinforcing.

6. **Extracting a Confession**: There is a tendency for some teachers to have a student admit or describe the misbehavior that led to time-out. This frequently happens when a student leaves time-out. A teacher may want students to acknowledge their misbehavior or to problem-solve behavior alternatives. Unfortunately, "extracting a confession" reduces the effectiveness of time-out. If a teacher feels a need to

review the student's misbehavior after the time-out period, it is better to simply restate a precision command—"I need you not to . . . . (the misbehavior)" and leave it at that.

Legal Issues and Cautions

1. Informed consent must be obtained from a student's parent(s) or guardian(s) before a time-out room can be used. The procedures should be explained to the parents; they should be shown the time-out room and they should sign the "What is Time-Out?" form.

2. The behavior identified on the "What is Time-Out?" form for use with time-out rooms should be serious or very maladaptive behaviors (e.g., aggression, severe noncompliance, tantrums, property destruction). For less serious behaviors (e.g., crying, whining, talking out in class), other, less intrusive procedures should be used.

3. When a time-out room is used, there should be a time-out log on which to record target behavior, time in, and time out. This log should be filled out, signed, and dated by a staff member each time the room is used.

4. A time-out room should never be frightening, dark, or unventilated. The time-out space should merely be boring.

5. A time-out room should always be fitted with a window or peep hole so the student can be observed.

6. A person should always be outside of the room and should never leave while the room is in use.

7. Items such as belts, shoes, or the contents of pockets (e.g., pencils, pens, paper clips, or knives) should be removed when a time-out room is used for students with severe behavioral disorders.

8. Excessively long durations should not be used with time-out. For most students, one minute per year of age is a reasonable guideline. Time periods should always be decided upon by the IEP team before the procedure is actually used because angry adults tend to use excessively long periods of time.

9. It is always best to use a time-out room door which the student can push open from the inside and exit if the door is left unattended by an adult.

10. Assess all staff's knowledge concerning the use of time-out and keep the results on file to document that all staff have been trained.

11. Post the time-out procedures on the time-out room door.

The Dos and Don'ts of Time-out

1. Do explain the total procedure to the student before implementing time-out. Don't start the procedure without first explaining time-out to the student in a calm, unemotional manner.

2. Do prepare a time-out setting for the student which is clean, well lighted, and ventilated. Don't just pick any available location. Make sure that it isn't dark, too confining, dangerous, or not ventilated.

3. Do pick a place or situation for time-out that is boring and less reinforcing than the classroom. Don't pick a place that is scary or more reinforcing than the classroom (for example, sitting in the hall).

4. Do use a set of structured verbal requests with a student such as the recommended precision request format described in a previous module of this book. Don't threaten a student repeatedly with time-out.

5. Do remain calm. Don't get into a verbal exchange with a student on the way to time-out, or while in time-out.

6. Do place a student in time-out for a set period of time which you control. Don't tell a student to come out of time-out when he/she is "ready to behave."

7. Do require the student to be quiet for 30 seconds at the end of the time-out period, before they are let out. Don't let a student out of time-out while he/she is crying, screaming, yelling, or tantruming.

8. Do use shorter periods of time for time-out; one minute per year of age is a good guideline. Don't use excessively long periods of time.

9. Do require the student to complete the request that led to time-out, or to complete any academic work missed while he/she was in time-out. Don't allow a student to avoid compliance with a request or to miss academic work by going to time-out.

10. Do have someone responsible for the student during time-out, preferably equipped with an audible signaling device (egg timer) to let them know when the student should exit. Don't put a student in time-out without a responsible person checking on the student or knowing what to do in an emergency.

11. Do ignore a student who says he/she likes time-out or will not come out of time-out. Don't beg a student to come out of time-out.

12. Do make a student clean up a mess that is made in time-out. Don't let a student make a mess in the time-out room and avoid cleaning it.

13. Do add to the length of time-out for each request you have to make to a student who refuses to go to time-out. Don't threaten, yell, beg, or fight with a student to get them to go to time-out.

14. Do keep data on the use of time-out such as: who is responsible for the student, time in and time out, reason for being placed in time-out, and date. Don't assume you can remember these details at a later date or that you don't need the data.

15. Do write down the basic steps and procedures on how to use time-out in your school, have the staff read them, and post them along with the time-out log on the door of the time-out room.

16. Do get parent(s)' permission before you use a time-out room: Show them the time-out room, have them sign a permission sheet, have them read the time-out procedures, and include it in the student's Individualized Education Plan (IEP). Don't assume it is all right with the parent(s) if you use the procedures, or that it doesn't need to be included on an IEP.

17. Do change the time-out procedure or parameters (length of time, place, or type of time-out) if the data indicate that it is not working over a reasonable period of time (two weeks). Don't assume that time-out will work for every student, or for all types of inappropriate behaviors, in all types of settings.

References

Foxx, R.M. & Shapiro, S.T. (1978). The time-out ribbon: A non-exclusionary time-out procedure. *Journal of Applied Behavior Analysis, 11*, 125-136.

Recommended Resources

Bean, A.W. & Roberts, M.W. (1981). The effect to time-out release contingencies on changes in child noncompliance. *Journal of Abnormal Child Psychology, 9*, 95-105.

Brantner, J. & Doherty, M.A. (1983). A review of time-out: A conceptual and methodological analysis. In A. Axelrod & J. Apsche (Eds.), *The effects of punishment on human behavior*. New York: Academic Press.

Burleigh, R. & Maroholin, D., II, (1977). Don't shoot until you see the whites of his eyes: An analysis of the adverse side effects of verbal prompts. *Behavior Modification, 1*, 109-122.

Cuenin, L.H. & Harris, K.R. (1986). Planning, implementing, and evaluating time-out interventions with exceptional students. *Teaching Exceptional Children, 18*(4), 272-276.

Drabman, R.S. & Creedon, D.L. (1979). "Marking time-out:" A procedure for away from home. *Child and Behavior Therapy, 1*, 99-101.

Firestone, P. (1976). The effects and side effects of time-out on an aggressive nursery school child. *Journal of Behavior Therapy and Experimental Psychiatry, 6*, 79-81.

Gast, D.L. & Nelson, C.M. (1977). Legal and ethical considerations for the use of time-out in special education settings. *Journal of Special Education, 11*, 457-467.

Harris, K. (1985). Definitional, parametric, and procedural considerations in time-out interventions and research. *Exceptional Children, 5*(1), 279-288.

Hobbs, S.A. & Forehand, R. (1977). Important parameters in the use of time-out on children's deviant behavior. *Journal of Behavior Therapy and Experimental Psychiatry, 8*, 365-370.

Nelson, M.C. & Rutherford, R.B. (1983). Time-out revisited and its use in special education. *Exceptional Education Quarterly, 3*, 56-67.

Roberts, M.W., Hatzenbuehler, L.C., & Bean, A.W. (1981). The effects of differential attention and time-out on child noncompliance. *Behavior Therapy, 12*, 93-99.

Roberts, M.W. (1982). The effects of warned versus unwarned time-out procedures on child noncompliance. *Child and Family Behavior Therapy, 4*, 37-53.

Rolider, A. & Van Houten, R. (1985a). Movement suppression time-out for undesirable behavior in psychotic and severely developmentally delayed children. *Journal of Applied Behavior Analysis, 8,* 275-268.

Rolider, A. & Van Houten, R. (1985b). Suppressing tantrum behavior in public places through the use of delayed punishment mediated by audio recordings. *Behavior Therapy, 16,* 181-194.

Sign, N.N., Beale, I.L., & Dawson, M.J. (1981). Duration of facial screening and suppression of self-injurious behavior: Analysis using an alternating treatments design. *Behavioral Assessment, 3,* 411-420.

Sign, N.N., Winton, A.S.W., & Dawson, M.J. (1982). The suppression of antisocial behavior by facial screening using multiple-baseline and alternating treatment designs. *Behavior Therapy, 13,* 511-520.

Van Houten, R. & Rolider, A. (1988). Recreating the scene: An effective way to provide delayed punishment for inappropriate motor behavior. *Journal of Applied Behavior Analysis, 21*(2), 187-192.

Zabel, M.K. (1986). Time-out use with behaviorally disordered students. *Behavior Disorders, 12,* 15-21.

Davis School District
Approved Time-Out Room Policy and Procedures

Written by Ginger Rhode and Melisa Genaux

Introduction

The Davis School District Time-Out Room Policy and Procedures is in compliance with the Utah State Office of Education policy on "Selection of Least Restrictive Behavioral Interventions (LRBI) for Use with Students with Disabilities." This document provides administrators, teachers, and parents with specific parameters for the use of time-out in the school setting. Time-out should be used only as one part of a comprehensive behavior management plan which includes high rates of positive reinforcement for appropriate behavior. This plan must be developed and approved through the IEP process.

Time-out is a shortened form of the term "time-out from positive reinforcement." The idea of time-out is to remove the student from an activity which is reinforcing (one which he/she enjoys) and to place him/her in an environment which provides no reinforcement. The procedure is very much like having a child sit in a chair at home for a short period of time as a consequence for misbehavior. There are a number of ways time-out can be used, ranging from non-exclusionary time-out procedures (e.g., planned ignoring, withdrawal of materials, seat away) to exclusionary time-out procedures (e.g., time-out in another classroom, time-out in a time-out room). For the purpose of this policy, the term "time-out" will refer exclusively to time-out in a time-out room.

Time-out is widely recognized as an effective intervention for decreasing the frequency of severe problem behaviors, such as physical aggression toward others or objects. Extensive research has shown that in order to maximize the procedure's effectiveness, a high rate of reinforcement must be available in the instructional setting. It is also important that students not be allowed to avoid tasks by going to time-out and that reinforcement is not available during the time-out period. This is why it is not advisable to use a child's bedroom at home or the hall or office at school for time-out.

Definition

Time-out is a behavior reductive technique for use with severe misbehavior. Its purpose is to reduce the severity, intensity, and/or likelihood of the misbehavior in the future. The procedure consists of removing a student from an environment which provides reinforcement to one which provides no reinforcement.

Use of Time-Out

1. Time-out must be used only for the most severe behaviors (e.g., physical aggression toward others or objects, extreme noncompliance) and only after positive intervention procedures have been tried and found to be unsuccessful. The procedure must never be used for minor inappropriate behaviors (e.g., talking out, off-task).

2. As a Level III intervention within the LRBI policy, time-out in a time-out room requires permission of Davis School District's Local Human Rights Committee prior to its implementation.

3. Prior written parental permission is also required before using a time-out room. Parents must sign the LRBI "Behavioral Interventions Consent Form," to which is attached the "Time-Out Information for Parents" form. The signed LRBI form and "Time-Out Information for Parents" form must be attached to the student's IEP.

4. All teachers and instructional assistants using time-out must be trained in advance and must complete the "Time-out Room Test." A copy of each staff member's test

must be kept on file and periodically reviewed with him/her.

5. The specific target behavior(s) for which time-out will be used must be defined on the LRBI "Behavioral Interventions Consent Form." Appropriate behaviors which will replace the behavior targeted for reduction must also be defined on the form. Systematic reinforcement must be implemented to increase the frequency of the replacement behaviors. Social skills training must be provided to enhance the student's repertoire of appropriate behavior.

6. Data must be collected on the target behavior in order to assess the effectiveness of the time-out procedure. All data collection must include a baseline measure (the rate of the behavior before an intervention is implemented).

7. The length of time-out must be specified in advance. Generally, one minute per year of age of the student is appropriate (e.g., six minutes for a six-year old student, ten minutes for a ten-year old student). Under no circumstances must a student be told to go to time-out and to come out when he/she can behave. The staff member in charge must always determine the length of the time-out period.

8. The "Davis School District Time-out Room Policy and Procedures" must be posted in the classroom as well as on or near the time-out room.

9. An adult must be in the same room or in relatively close proximity to the time-out room during the entire time-out procedure and must make frequent visual checks to ensure student safety and to monitor student behavior.

10. If a student urinates or defecates while in the time-out room, it is customary for him/her to clean the room under adult supervision at the end of the time-out period.

11. If a student damages the time-out room, it is customary for the parent(s) to be consulted and arrangements made for the student to assist in restitution.

Procedures

1. Before beginning to use time-out as a management procedure, identify and operationalize the behavior(s) which will result in its use. Be sure the student is afforded due process by explaining the behavior to him/her ahead of time. An explanation of the behavior may consist of telling the student, demonstrating the behavior, providing feedback, and answering any questions the student may have. The student must also be told how long the time-out period will last.

2. If the misbehavior occurs, identify it. Tell the student in a calm, neutral manner: "That's fighting; you need to go to time-out." Tell the student to remove jewelry, belt, and shoes. Tell the student to empty pockets (in order to check for such items as pens, pencils, paper clips, knives, etc.). Socks should be checked for these types of items also. If the student does not comply with the request to empty pockets, ask for back-up and empty the pockets yourself. No other conversation should ensue. Ignore any questions or any statements the student may make as an excuse for misbehavior. If you encounter resistance from the student, you should:

   a. Gently but firmly lead the student to the time-out room.

   b. At the end of the time-out period, require the student to clean up any mess resulting from resistance to time-out before he/she may return to classroom activities.

   c. Be prepared to add to the time-out period if the student refuses to go or is physically aggressive (hits, kicks, turns over furniture, etc.). Add one minute to the time, up to two additional minutes. If the student continues to refuse at this point, request help from back-up staff to place the student in time-out. It may be useful to plan a one-word signal ahead of time to communicate to staff that help is needed immediately.

3. Once a student enters the time-out room, the time begins. Check the clock or set a timer. Release from time-out is contingent upon a minimum duration of time-out (generally one minute per year of age). Furthermore, the student is not released from time-out until he/she has had a short quiet time (generally 30-60 seconds) at the end of the time-out period. The IEP team will always make a final determination as to what is an appropriate minimum duration of time-out, as well as the amount of required quiet time for each student.

4. As a rule, a student should not spend more than 55 consecutive minutes in time-out for each occurrence of the targeted behavior. Any time-out period which exceeds 55 minutes must adhere to the Process for Implementation of Emergency Procedures outlined in the LRBI policy. **Caution:** Anytime a time-out period exceeds 55 minutes, the parents and special education director must be notified within 24 hours.

5. Once the time-out period has ended, return the student to the ongoing classroom activity, making sure the student is required to complete the task in which he/she was engaged prior to the time-out period. This will ensure that students do not purposely avoid unpleasant tasks by going to time-out. Do not ask the student why he/she needed to go to time-out. Do not comment at this time on how well the student behaved while in time-out. Doing so is likely to reinforce the student's behavior and is likely to result in an increase in the behaviors targeted for reduction with time-out.

At a later time, when the student is behaving appropriately, an adult may review with him/her a description of the inappropriate behavior that resulted in time-out, the appropriate behavior that should have been exhibited, and a rationale for exhibiting the appropriate behavior. An opportunity to role play and practice the appropriate behavior a number of times is recommended, with feedback, coaching, and reinforcement from the adult.

6. Record the use of time-out on the "Time-Out Room Log." The log must be posted on or near the time-out room door and must include the following information:

a. The student's name

b. The date the procedure was used

c. The behavior resulting in time-out

d. The time the student was placed in time-out

e. The time the student was released from time-out

f. The total time the student spent in time-out

g. The student's behavior while in time-out

h. The initials of the staff member who placed the student in time-out

i. The initials of the staff member who supervised the student in time-out, if this is a different individual from the one who placed the student in time-out

A cover sheet must be in place over the "Time-Out Room Log" to prevent the observation of written documentation of time-out activities by casual observers or by visitors to the educational setting.

7. Graph time-out data, and review them often (on at least a weekly basis) to determine the effectiveness of the time-out procedure. With input from team members, adjust the IEP behavior management plan accordingly. Scheduled intervention review dates will be specified by the Davis School District Local Human Rights Committee.

8. In the event of an emergency (e.g., fire or fire drill), the adult supervising the time-out must abort the time-out procedure. The adult will supervise the student in following normal classroom/school procedures under such conditions.

Behavioral Interventions Consent Form

Student Name: _____ Date: _____

School: _____ Grade: _____ Date of Birth: _____

1. Target Behavior (operational definition): _____

   _____

   _____

   _____

   _____

   Baseline Date: _____

   Summarize Data and Attach Data Sheets: _____

   _____

   _____

2. Replacement Behavior (operational definition): _____

   _____

   _____

   _____

   _____

   Baseline Date: _____

   Summarize Data and Attach Data Sheets: _____

   _____

3. Documentation of Level I and II interventions used unsuccessfully (attach data sheets):

   _____

   _____

   _____

4. Corresponding IEP Goal and/or Terminal Objective: _____

   _____

   _____

   _____

5. Recommended Behavioral Intervention Procedures:

   A. Appropriate behavior to increase and positive reinforcement methods/schedule:

   _____

   _____

   _____

   B. Recommended behavior reduction procedures:_____

   _____

   The level this procedure falls under:_____

   C. Specifically describe the Intrusive Procedure (attach a written program if necessary):

   _____

   _____

   _____

   _____

6. Data Collection (summarize method and schedule): _____

   _____

   _____

7. Scheduled Intervention Review date:_____

8. Cautions or Side Effects: _____

   _____

   _____

   _____

   _____

I have read the above information and hereby give my informed consent for the specific procedures to be used with the target student. (All must sign and date.)

_____
(parent/guardian signature)   (date)

_____
(teacher's signature)   (date)

_____
(administrator's signature)   (date)

Time-Out Information for Parents

Time-out is a technique that is used to decrease the frequency of severe problem behaviors such as physical aggression toward others or objects. The procedure is very much like having your child sit in a chair at home for a short period of time as a consequence for misbehavior. The idea of time-out is to remove the student from an activity or environment that is reinforcing (one which he/she enjoys) and to place him/her in an environment that provides no reinforcement. For example, if the student is in the classroom where praise and tokens or points may be earned for appropriate behavior and he/she hits another student, he/she would be removed immediately to a time-out room (where no reinforcers may be earned) for a specified period of time.

The length of the time-out period is set in advance. Generally, one minute per year of age of the student is appropriate (e.g. six minutes for a six-year old student, ten minutes for a ten-year old student). A quiet time (usually 30-60 seconds) is required at the end of the time-out period before the student is released to return to the classroom activity. These times are determined by the IEP team prior to the use of time-out. The frequency of needed visual checks for the student in time-out is also discussed by the IEP team. Particularly when time-out is first used, it may take longer than the predetermined time-out period to get the required amount of quiet time. Anytime a time-out period exceeds 55 minutes, you will be notified by the school staff within 24 hours. In such cases, it is Davis School District's policy to adhere to the Process for Implementation of Emergency Procedures as specified by the Utah State Office of Education's Least Restrictive Behavior Intervention (LRBI) Policy. If such an occurrence takes place more than once in a week, two times in a month, or a total of four times in a year, it will be addressed by reconvening the IEP team and by following the Davis School District Local Human Rights Committee procedures.

The effectiveness of time-out will be systematically and objectively assessed on an ongoing basis. You may request a review of the time-out intervention effectiveness at any time.

A staff member is always in attendance when time-out is used. A detailed log of all time-out periods is kept to record the behavior that resulted in the time-out, the date and time the student is placed in time-out, the length of the time-out period, and the student's behavior while in time-out.

Possible Side Effects

- Some students may find isolation in a time-out room reinforcing.

- A student may become aggressive or injure himself/herself or school personnel when being taken to a time-out room or while in the time-out room.

Student Name _____

Length of time-out period _____ min.

Length of quiet time _____ sec.

Parent has received a copy of the Davis School District Time-Out Room Policy and Procedures.

_____
(parent signature)

_____
(date)

Time-Out Room Log

Student's Name	Date	Target Behavior	Time In	Time Out	Staff	Comments

Time-Out Test

(Mark each statement True or False.)

	True	False
1. It is appropriate to use time-out for off-task behavior if it is a severe problem.		
2. When a student is sent to time-out, he/she should be told, "You may come out when you can behave."		
3. An adult must be in attendance during the entire time-out procedure.		
4. After a student is told to go to time-out, the teacher should immediately empty the student's pockets.		
5. A student should be required, after the time-out period is over, to clean up any mess resulting from resistance to time-out.		
6. If a student refuses to go to time-out, one minute should be added to the time, up to ten additional minutes.		
7. If the time-out period exceeds 55 minutes more than two times in one month, the IEP team should be consulted about an alternative plan of action.		
8. After the time-out period has ended, the student should be returned to the activity in which he/she was engaged before time-out.		
9. It is appropriate to use the school office, but not the hall, for time-out.		
10. Time-out should be considered one part of a comprehensive behavior management plan which includes high rates of positive reinforcement for appropriate behavior.		
11. It is all right to use time-out without parental permission in emergency situations.		
12. Behaviors which are incompatible with those resulting in time-out must be defined and systematically reinforced.		
13. All data collection should include a baseline measure.		
14. The "Davis School District Time-out Room Policy and Procedures" should be posted in the classroom and on or near the time-out room.		
15. If a student argues about the misbehavior on the way to the time-out room, the teacher should keep explaining in a calm manner why the student needs to go to time-out.		

Other Sopris West
Publications of Interest

The Tough Kid Book: Practical Classroom Management Strategies

by Ginger Rhode • William R. Jenson • H. Kenton Reavis

If you are preparing to teach—and thus work with "Tough Kids"—*The Tough Kid Book* will be a survival manual for your first years of teaching. If you are a practicing teacher, this is a resource they should have used when you were in college. With over 100,000 copies in print, the wildly popular *The Tough Kid Book* has become an indispensable resource for both regular and special education teachers. The research-validated solutions included in this book help to reduce disruptive behavior in Tough Kids without big investments of the teacher's time, money, or emotions. These solutions also provide Tough Kids with behavioral, academic, and social survival skills. This book contains a wealth of ready to use strategies and identifies other commercially available, practical resources for teachers who want even more in-depth assistance. 120 pages.

The Tough Kid Tool Box

by William R. Jenson • Ginger Rhode • H. Kenton Reavis

The Tough Kid Tool Box provides elementary and middle school teachers with straightforward, classroom-tested, ready to use materials for managing and motivating tough to teach students. *The Tough Kid Book* readers will recognize such gems as: Behavior Observation Forms; Mystery Motivator Charts; Reward Spinners; Icon "Countoons" for Self-Monitoring; Classroom Contracts; Reinforcer Lists; Point Cards; Classroom Activity Schedules for Maximum Engaged Time; and many, many more. 214 pages.

Homework Teams: Homework Management Strategies for the Classroom

by Daniel Olympia • Debra Andrews • Lane Valum • William Jenson

This manual guides teachers in establishing a homework program that essentially runs itself! The process is based on cooperative learning teams with a group contingency reward system. In some classes, *Homework Teams* has raised classroom homework completion rates from 35% to 80%! 76 pages.

Strategies and Tactics for Effective Instruction (STEI)

by Bob Algozzine • James Ysseldyke

Effective teaching is a complex process. Research has shown that there are effective ways to plan, manage, deliver, and evaluate instruction. Yet, tactics that work with some students often do not work with others. Teachers will find *STEI* a treasure chest of information on teaching tactics that work. 210 pages.

TGIF: But What Will I Do on Monday?

by Susan L. Fister • Karen A. Kemp

A powerful resource for educators—working alone or collaboratively—seeking quick, effective instructional modification procedures for accommodating all students. These practical techniques respond to needs encountered at four critical points in the instructional process: Teacher-Directed Instruction; Guided Practice Activities; Independent Practice Activities; and Final Measurement.

Organized in a quick reference format, the TGIF system allows educators to easily identify the specific challenge they face, locate the most appropriate question under one of the four instructional component headings, and select one of the many research-based techniques listed. 178 pages.

TGIF: Making It Work on Monday

by Susan L. Fister • Karen A. Kemp

A companion to the popular *TGIF: But What Will I Do on Monday?*. Filled with valuable materials for teachers and students, this book of 100 blackline masters includes tracking sheets, organizing forms, handouts, and activity sheets which make the accommodations in *TGIF* easy to implement. Teachers save precious planning time with these ready to use activities and ideas. 204 pages.

For ordering information call   **(800) 547-6747**
or visit our website   **www.sopriswest.com**